D0322903

Themed Activities for People with Learning Difficulties

Themed Activities for People with Learning Difficulties

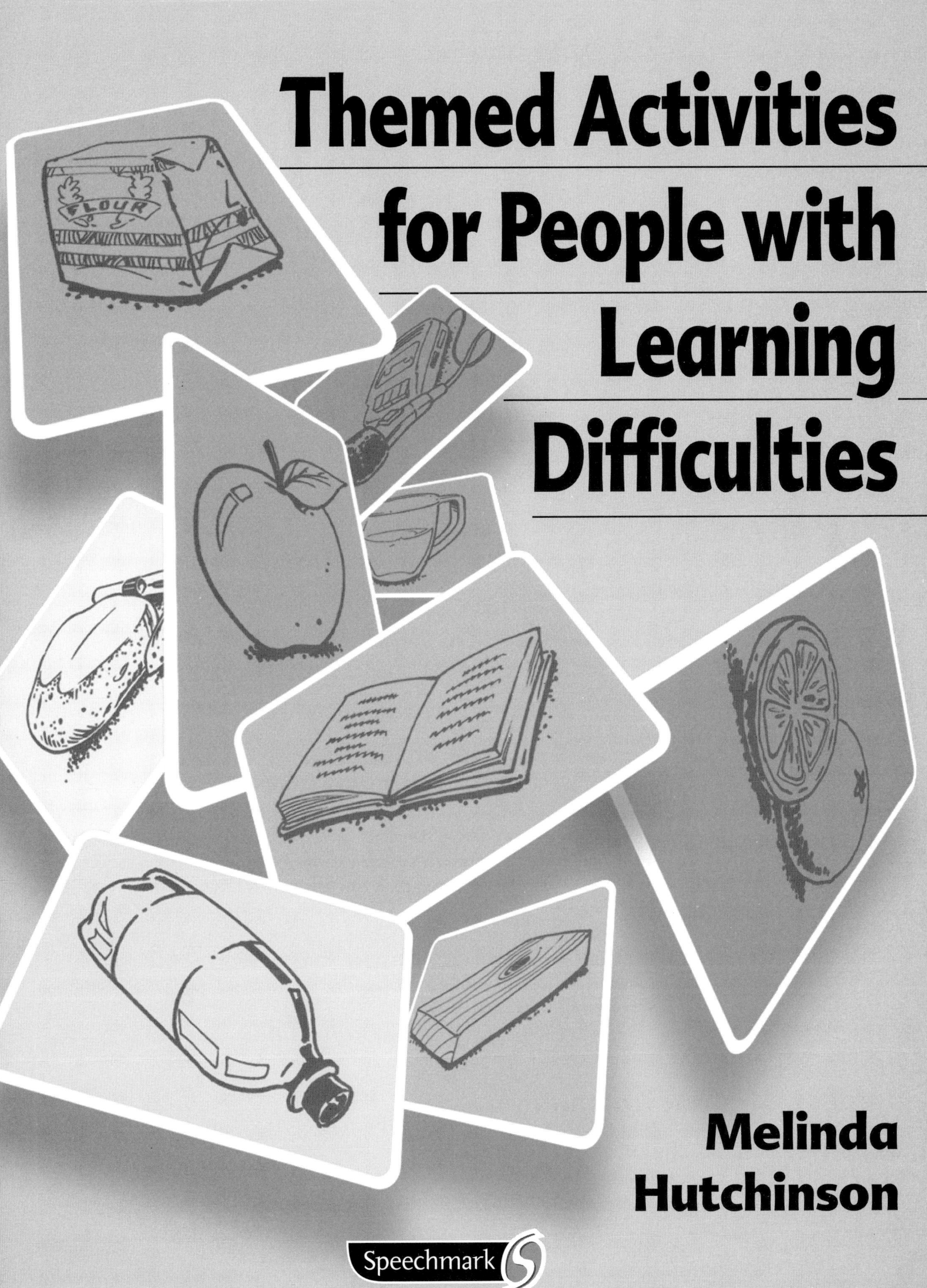

Melinda Hutchinson

Speechmark

www.speechmark.net

This book is dedicated to my parents, for their continual encouragement and belief in me, Freda Abbro who shared her dream, and Julie Williams for her friendship.

First published in 2003.

Speechmark Publishing Ltd, 70 Alston Drive, Bradwell Abbey, Milton Keynes MK13 9HG, UK
Tel: +44 (0)1908 326944 Fax: +44 (0)1908 326960
www.speechmark.net

© Melinda Hutchinson, 2003

Reprinted 2005, 2008

All rights reserved. The whole of this work, including all text and illustrations, is protected by copyright. No part of it may be copied, altered, adapted or otherwise exploited in any way without express prior permission, unless it is in accordance with the provisions of the Copyright Designs and Patents Act 1988 or in order to photocopy or make duplicating masters of those pages so indicated, without alteration and including copyright notices, for the express purposes of instruction and examination. No parts of this work may otherwise be loaded, stored, manipulated, reproduced, or transmitted in any form or by any means, electronic or mechanical, including photocopying and recording, or by any information storage and retrieval system without prior written permission from the publisher, on behalf of the copyright owner.

002-4789/Printed in the United Kingdom/1030

British Library Cataloguing in Publication Data
Hutchinson, Melinda
Themed activities for people with learning difficulties
1. Learning disabled – Education 2. Problem solving – Study and teaching
3. Creativity – Study and teaching 4. Special education – Activity programs
I. Title

ISBN: 978 0 86388 307 1

Contents

FIGURES

TABLES

Acknowledgements

I should like to thank all the students with whom I have worked over the years for their inspirational contributions and suggestions, which have helped to form the contents and format of this book.

Additional thanks go to Caroline Allen, the staff and governors at Orchard Hill College of Further Education; Mark Gray (RNIB); Carolyn Greenwood; family and friends, and all those who have provided guidance and support.

Introduction

To be 'creative' is not just being 'artistic' – it is also about exploration, discovery and solving problems. With the opportunity of participation, learners with profound and complex learning difficulties can build on existing and new experiences to develop and practise new and familiar skills.

When asked to be 'creative', many of us automatically think of art-related activities such as painting or drawing. Our own memories of success and failure will have a bearing on how we, as professionals, may approach this area of 'being creative'. If we are reluctant to experience new areas and approaches, we will reduce the opportunities of those we work with. It is hoped that the ideas in this book will provide a starting point for those who feel uncertain in this area, or do not have the time to research topics. This will involve a certain amount of risk-taking for both the learners and those working with them as new areas are explored.

The focus of the book is to provide a practical approach to object-based activities with resource materials, ideas and flexible structures to extend and complement professionals' existing approaches. It also aims to develop the inclusion of learners' ideas and needs into activities, as each individual contribution to an activity is valid and important and should be acknowledged and respected as such. The book will look at a range of teaching approaches, ideas for adapting activities and equipment, and how to present materials and tasks to the learner.

This is a resource book providing ideas, work outlines, activities and methods, recording sheets and photocopiable materials. It is aimed at those working with people with profound and complex learning difficulties in a variety of settings, including educational establishments, day provisions and at home.

The book looks at 20 objects – each in four different ways through various activities. Each activity has focus objectives and a recording sheet. The activities can be used on an individual basis, in a group setting, or both. Each activity has been designed to provide opportunities for participation at all ability levels, and it is possible for each learner to take part in an activity, however small that involvement may be. Individuals can participate on a passive level as well as on a more physical and intellectual one. To experience an activity or a part of an activity with or without assistance is a very important learning opportunity. Contributions to an activity should be directed by the needs and abilities of the learner, with assistance, where required, from those facilitating.

By using the focus objective sheets, the activities can be broken down into achievable stages, or linked into ongoing objectives. Some learners will complete activities with minimal guidance, while others will need varying degrees of assistance to access some parts or all of the activities. The focus objectives and recording sheets for each activity are intended as guidelines. How those are developed will depend on individual situations and needs.

Blank theme boxes, recording sheets, data sheets, and information about materials and resources are also included. These are provided as starting points and will most likely need to be adapted to the needs of individual learners.

It is hoped that those who use this book will be able to develop their own themes, experiences and confidence, and in so doing develop and create personalised resources that reflect the contributions made by all those who have participated. The objects used in the book are examples of how we can look at objects in different ways – the list is endless. The challenge is to look at everyday objects in different ways, and through a shared exploration make new discoveries.

How to use this book

The Contents page lists all the themes that have focus objectives, activity outlines and recording sheets. The activities for each theme can be used as part of a four-part project or as individual activities. Additional blank forms and resource ideas are also included in the book.

1 Choosing a theme

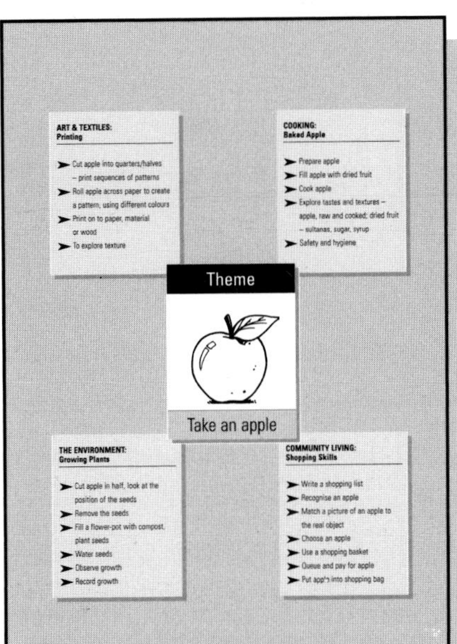

2 Choosing an activity

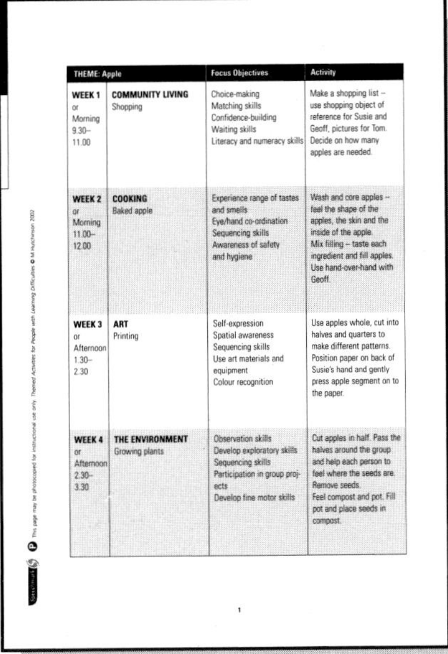

THEME: Apple		Focus Objectives	Activity
WEEK 1 or Morning 9.30–11.00	COMMUNITY LIVING Shopping	Choice-making Matching skills Confidence-building Waiting skills Literacy and numeracy skills	Make a shopping list – use shopping object of reference for Susie and Geoff, pictures for Tom. Decide on how many apples are needed.
WEEK 2 or Morning 11.00–12.00	COOKING Baked apple	Experience range of tastes and smells Eye/hand co-ordination Sequencing skills Awareness of safety and hygiene	Wash and core apples – feel the shape of the apples, the skin and the inside of the apple. Mix filling – taste each ingredient and fill apples. Use hand-over-hand with Geoff.
WEEK 3 or Afternoon 1.30–2.30	ART Printing	Self-expression Spatial awareness Sequencing skills Use art materials and equipment Colour recognition	Use apples whole, cut into halves and quarters to make different patterns. Position paper on back of Susie's hand and gently press apple segment on to the paper.
WEEK 4 or Afternoon 2.30–3.30	THE ENVIRONMENT Growing plants	Observation skills Develop exploratory skills Sequencing skills Participation in group projects Develop fine motor skills	Cut apples in half. Pass the halves around the group and help each person to feel where the seeds are. Remove seeds. Feel compost and pot. Fill pot and place seeds in compost.

1

3 Activity checklist

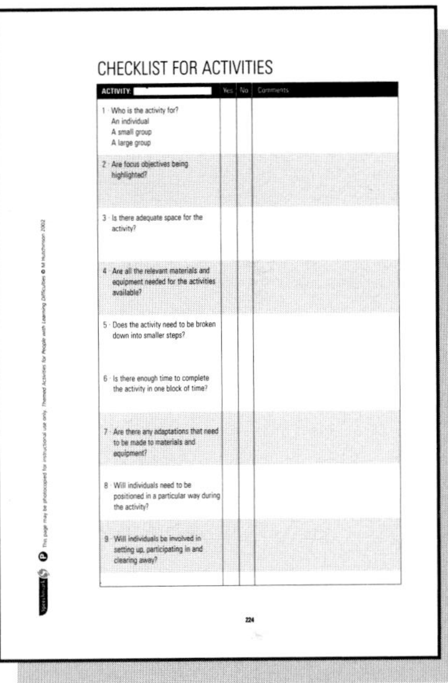

CHECKLIST FOR ACTIVITIES

ACTIVITY	Yes	No	Comments
1 Who is the activity for? An individual / A small group / A large group			
2 Are focus objectives being highlighted?			
3 Is there adequate space for the activity?			
4 Are all the relevant materials and equipment needed for the activities available?			
5 Does the activity need to be broken down into smaller steps?			
6 Is there enough time to complete the activity in one block of time?			
7 Are there any adaptations that need to be made to materials and equipment?			
8 Will individuals need to be positioned in a particular way during the activity?			
9 Will individuals be involved in setting up, participating in and clearing away?			

224

4 Activity plan

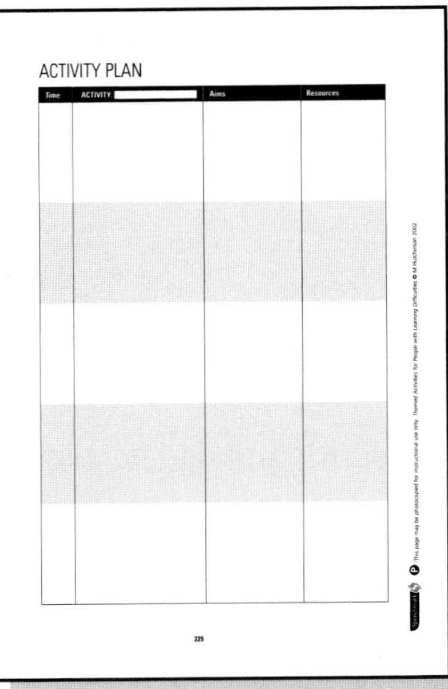

ACTIVITY PLAN

Time	ACTIVITY	Aims	Resources

225

5 Recording sheet

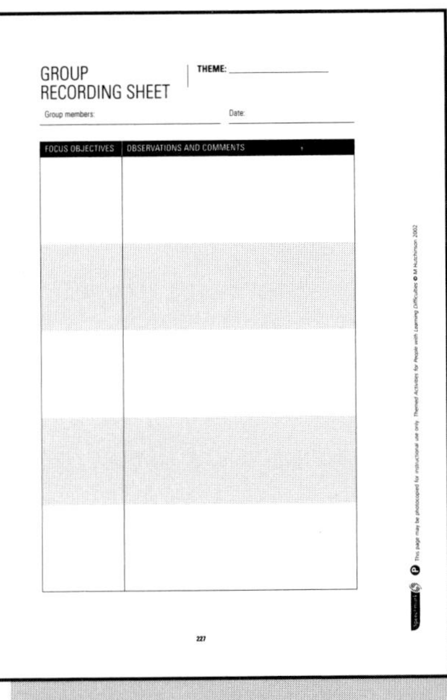

GROUP RECORDING SHEET | THEME:

Group members: Date:

FOCUS OBJECTIVES	OBSERVATIONS AND COMMENTS

227

6 Evaluation sheet

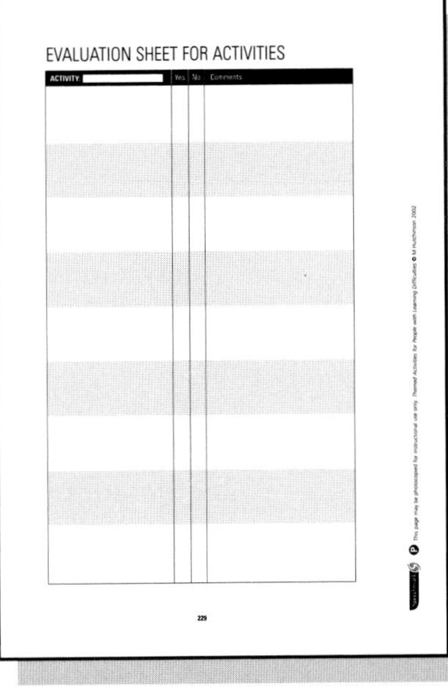

EVALUATION SHEET FOR ACTIVITIES

ACTIVITY	Yes	No	Comments

229

1 Choosing a Theme

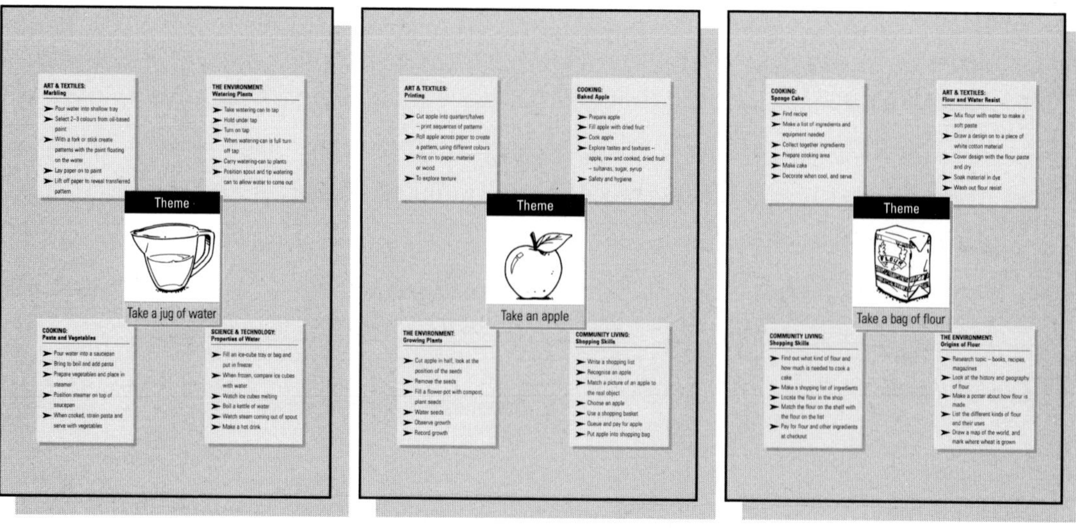

FIGURE 1 · **CHOOSING A THEME**

Themes can provide a structured starting point from which to expand and develop experiences. By using everyday objects in a variety of contexts, learners with profound and complex learning difficulties can build up a relevant picture of the world around them. Some examples are shown in Figure 1.

Before choosing a theme, it is important to look at the individual needs and interests of the learner or group. It is also necessary to consider the following areas:

- Staffing
- Where the activity will take place
- What resources will be needed
- Funding
- Transport

The intention of this book is to provide ideas that focus on everyday objects and how they can be used in a variety of ways. Hopefully this will keep down costs and solve some of the problems that arise from a lack of appropriate and relevant resources.

It may appear difficult to choose a theme or activity that will suit and benefit the different needs and abilities of each person in a group setting. Some activities will be seen as too advanced for some learners, or not appropriate in some way. However, it is not the activity that is the focus, but how it is approached and presented to each individual in the group. Therefore, it is possible to use one activity for a group with a diverse range of abilities.

Figure 2 aims to show how this can be achieved using the activities in the book. It describes a small group of learners whose needs and abilities vary.

EXAMPLE GROUP

SUSIE is non-ambulant and sits in her wheelchair in a semi-reclined position. She has minimal use of her arms and hands and requires assistance to hold and touch objects. Susie has good eyesight and will visually track movement and objects. She reacts to voices and sounds by turning towards the source of the sound and responding with vocalisations.

TOM has some verbal language. He will say his name, verbally recognise objects such as cup, scissors, pen; count to five, repeat individual words unfamiliar to him. He is mobile and has good fine motor skills. Tom visually recognises others in the group, but prefers to sit alone.

GEOFF has a visual impairment. He responds to movement, contrast and strong light sources. Geoff will reach out with his hands to locate people and objects. He requires assistance to do this and has his hands guided through parts of activities – holding a glue stick and putting glue on to paper, for example. Geoff uses touch to communicate his needs to others, and will use objects as a reference point.

FIGURE 2 · **A GROUP OF LEARNERS WITH VARYING ABILITIES**

For the learners in Figure 2, the art activity from the 'Take an apple' theme will provide opportunities for Susie to experience a range of textures and smells, and to develop her communication skills using eye-pointing. For Tom, the art activity will offer situations within which he can extend his vocabulary and build on numeracy skills. Geoff will benefit from one-to-one time with staff to develop his communication skills through using objects of reference, and to encourage him to use his residual vision.

The group will be used as an example of how to select, plan, execute, record and evaluate an activity.

2 Choosing an Activity

Table 1 shows how each theme can be followed as a block of four linked activities over a set period of time – for example, over four weeks or through a day, or as 'one off' activities. Individual situations will determine how much time is spent on each activity. Flexible timescales will create environments that can expand and incorporate ideas and approaches from both the learner and the facilitator.

THEME: Apple		Focus Objectives	Activity
WEEK 1 or Morning 9.30–11.00	**COMMUNITY LIVING** Shopping	Choice-making Matching skills Confidence-building Waiting skills Literacy and numeracy skills	Make a shopping list – use shopping object of reference for Susie and Geoff, pictures for Tom. Decide on how many apples are needed.
WEEK 2 or Morning 11.00–12.00	**COOKING** Baked apple	Experience range of tastes and smells Eye/hand co-ordination Sequencing skills Awareness of safety and hygiene	Wash and core apples – feel the shape of the apples, the skin and the inside of the apple. Mix filling – taste each ingredient and fill apples. Use hand-over-hand with Geoff.
WEEK 3 or Afternoon 1.30–2.30	**ART** Printing	Self-expression Spatial awareness Sequencing skills Use art materials and equipment Colour recognition	Use apples whole, cut into halves and quarters to make different patterns. Position paper on back of Susie's hand and gently press apple segment on to the paper.
WEEK 4 or Afternoon 2.30–3.30	**THE ENVIRONMENT** Growing plants	Observation skills Develop exploratory skills Sequencing skills Participation in group projects Develop fine motor skills	Cut apples in half. Pass the halves around the group and help each person to feel where the seeds are. Remove seeds. Feel compost and pot. Fill pot and place seeds in compost.

TABLE 1 · **FOLLOWING A THEME AS A BLOCK OF LINKED ACTIVITIES**

3 Activity Checklist

Having chosen an activity, a checklist needs to be drawn up to ensure that the appropriate equipment, materials, staffing, space and funds are available and accessible. Figure 3 is an example of a checklist.

ACTIVITY: Art: Printing	Yes	No	Comments
1 · Who is the activity for? An individual A small group A large group	 Yes		Small group: *Susie* – non-ambulant, minimal movement in arms and hands *Tom* – some verbal language and signing; uses scissors, etc independently *Geoff* – visual impairment – sees movement.
2 · Are focus objectives being highlighted?	Yes		Use focus objectives as an assessment for each person in the group.
3 · Is there adequate space for the activity?	Yes		Move the tables into the middle of the room to make room for Susie's wheelchair.
4 · Are all the relevant materials and equipment needed for the activities available?		No	Bring a chair that is familiar to Geoff (one with arms), to provide him with a feeling of security.
5 · Does the activity need to be broken down into smaller steps?		No	But will need to work one-to-one with Susie and Geoff.
6 · Is there enough time to complete the activity in one block of time?	Yes		Set up room and lay out materials before the activity is due to begin.
7 · Are there any adaptations that need to be made to materials and equipment?	Yes		Cover Geoff's table with a piece of black paper to make art equipment and materials stand out. Use an art board to go across Susie's lap to bring the materials within her reach.
8 · Will individuals need to be positioned in a particular way during the activity?	Yes		Geoff to sit with his back to the window to reduce glare from outside. Tom to sit near to the table with art materials and equipment on. Position Susie's wheelchair sideways on to the table.
9 · Will individuals be involved in setting up, participating in and clearing away?	Yes		Ask Tom to put the piece of black paper on Geoff's table. Give each person a specific item to put away.

FIGURE 3 · **A SAMPLE ACTIVITY CHECKLIST**

4 Activity Plan

The next stage after selecting a theme and time-scale is planning the activities. These do not need to be covered in the order in which they appear in the book, and can be rearranged to suit individual situations. Working from the activity checklist, build up a plan that will provide a flexible and accessible framework, as shown in Figure 4.

Time	ACTIVITY: Printing	Aims	Resources
9.00am	**Setting up the room** ➤ Position the tables in the middle of the room. ➤ Leave space for Susie's wheelchair to go sideways on to the table. ➤ Cover the tables with newspaper. ➤ Place art materials on a table near to the main tables. ➤ Position Geoff with his back to the window.	To provide a motivating and non-threatening environment. To accommodate individual needs through the presentation of the activity.	Apples Knife and board Overalls Art materials Tables and chairs Cassette player and quiet music Piece of black paper for Geoff Art board for Susie
9.30am	**Introducing the activity** ➤ When everyone is comfortably seated around the tables, pass the art object of reference around the group. ➤ After each person has felt and/or held the paintbrush, pass an apple around in the same way. ➤ Talk about using the apple with paint to make printed patterns on paper. ➤ Put on overalls in preparation for the activity.	To introduce the activity using objects. To allow time for individuals to explore objects linked to the activity. To encourage an awareness of others by passing objects.	Object of reference for art – paintbrush Apple to feel and smell Overalls
9.45am	**Activity: Printing with apples** ➤ Follow Worksheet 1	Refer to Focus Objectives on Worksheet 1	Refer to equipment list on Worksheet 1
10.45am	**Recording and evaluating** ➤ Complete the recording sheets either individually or as a group. ➤ Complete the evaluation sheet.	To record likes/dislikes. To acknowledge achievements.	Pens Recording sheets Evaluation sheet
11.30am	**Clearing away** ➤ Allocate an item for each person to put away.	To indicate the end of the activity.	Rubbish bin Cloth to wipe tables

FIGURE 4 · **A SAMPLE ACTIVITY PLAN**

5 Recording Sheets

Recording how an individual reacts to activities, uses equipment and relates to others is an important way of highlighting skills and progress. Filling in a recording sheet is not the only way to keep this information. Photographs, videos and audio tapes can be used as well completed pieces of work. However, it is important to keep written records as to how an individual is positioned; how they manipulate equipment; what communication methods they use, and what level of support they may need to complete activities. Figure 5 shows examples of a recording sheet.

RECORDING SHEET 1 | **THEME: TAKE AN APPLE** Printing

Name: Geoff Date: 3rd October

FOCUS OBJECTIVES	OBSERVATIONS AND COMMENTS
To encourage self-expression	Geoff held half a painted apple and tapped it twice on the paper independently after hands guided through – using left hand.
To develop spatial awareness	Required hands guided through to locate paper to print on to.
To develop sequencing skills	Repeated sequence of putting paint on apple with paintbrush with hands guided through.
To encourage exploration of the texture of art materials and equipment	Geoff spent up to a minute feeling and smelling the apple at the beginning of the activity. Geoff bit the apple. A print was made using the bitten piece of apple.
To develop colour recognition and matching	A black piece of paper positioned under Geoff's artwork made it easier for him to locate the white sheet of paper.

FIGURE 5 · **A SAMPLE RECORDING SHEET – INDIVIDUAL**

RECORDING SHEET 1 | **THEME: TAKE AN APPLE**
Printing

Group: Susie, Tom, Geoff

Date: 3rd October

FOCUS OBJECTIVES	OBSERVATIONS AND COMMENTS
To encourage self-expression	Everyone contributed to a group picture using own choice of apple segment.
To develop spatial awareness	Tom found spaces on the group picture to fill in. Susie and Geoff had help to position apple on paper.
To develop sequencing skills	The group were shown how to paint the apple and push segment on to the paper – repeated process.
To encourage exploration of the texture of art materials and equipment	Geoff and Susie needed more time than Tom to feel, hold and smell the apples and materials – Tom helped to pass items to the others.
To develop colour recognition and matching	Susie looked at the red paint longer than the blue on two occasions. Tom named all the colours used.

FIGURE 6 · **A SAMPLE RECORDING SHEET – GROUP**

The recording sheets in this book offer a suggested layout and content. Blank recording sheets are provided in the Appendices, which can be adapted to suit individuals and groups of learners.

6 Evaluation Sheet

Evaluating an activity provides important information about the learners' and facilitators' responses to the presentation and content of the activity. Involving both learners and staff in the evaluation process allows for change and adaptation to be made by everyone. Figure 7 is an example of an evaluation sheet for activities.

ACTIVITY: Art: Printing	Yes	No	Comments
1 · Was the activity appropriate?	Yes		Tom – 'I liked rolling the apple with paint on across the paper.' Susie and Tom both smiled when they smelt the apple.
2 · Were any highlighted focus objectives achieved?	Yes		Geoff independently made a print with the apple segment twice. Tom named all the colours of the paint used.
3 · Was the activity set up and presented appropriately?	Yes		The activity was explained clearly and staff understood the printing process. Useful to have a separate table with all the art materials on.
4 · Was there enough space for the activity?	Yes	No	Equipment was easily accessible. There was room to have Susie's wheelchair sideways on to the table. Tom – 'I wanted a table to myself.'
5 · Was the activity broken down into small enough stages?	Yes		Geoff had parts of the process repeated several times with his hands guided through.
6 · Was there enough time for the activity?	Yes		Plenty of time – even for exploring the different textures of the materials used.
7 · Were any adaptations to material or equipment successful?	Yes	No	The art board worked well with Susie – thought it might be too heavy. Geoff needed a lamp to highlight his work area, which was too dark
8 · Were individuals involved in all parts of the activity?	Yes	No	One-to-one ratio meant everyone was able to participate at their own pace. Susie and Geoff chose not to cut the apples.
9 · Are there any changes that need to be made for next time?	Yes		A lamp for Geoff. Position the tables so that they are connected, so that Tom has more space around him.

FIGURE 7 · **A SAMPLE EVALUATION SHEET FOR ACTIVITIES**

7 Teaching Approaches and Techniques

There are many approaches and techniques that can be used when delivering activities. The following are examples, which can be adapted or extended to benefit both learners and facilitators.

Prompts

Individuals will need varying amounts of assistance and guidance. A prompt offers support that can be gradually phased out until it is rarely or no longer required, as shown in Table 2.

Prompt abbreviation	Description of prompt	Individual's response to prompt	Assistance required
P	Passive	Watches, listens, smells, vocalises	Object held by staff
PP	Physical Prompt	Touches object	Hand and arm supported by staff
GP	Gestural Prompt	Reaches out to object	Sign 'look' and point at object
VP	Verbal Prompt	Follows verbal request to touch object	Repeat verbal request
I	Independently	Touches, reaches out to, picks up object with no prompts	None required after initial request

TABLE 2 · **SUPPORT OFFERED BY A PROMPT**

There will be situations where the use of verbal and gestural prompts will need to be used together to clarify a request. The abbreviations above may be used when recording information about an individual's participation in, or response to, an activity or object.

When using prompts it is important to

- Speak clearly, at a reasonable pace, and repeat instructions where necessary
- Gently hold under the wrist and forearm, or guide from the shoulder when providing physical support
- Link gestures with signing systems, and indicate with clear and exaggerated movements and facial expressions.

Demonstration

Beginning the activity with a demonstration is a useful way of providing both the learners and staff with an overview of the activity and what is expected of them. Each stage of an activity can also be demonstrated, to clarify the process and to encourage individuals to participate with more confidence.

Using cues

A cue provides a signal that reminds the individual of what comes next. Cues can be verbal, visual, an object, a sound, a name, a gesture, a picture or a person. Cues may need to be repeated during an activity to enable learners to participate and begin to initiate their own ideas.

Objects of reference

Objects can be used to represent an activity, a place, an object or a person. The objects need to be relevant to the individuals using them, and for practical reasons, cheap and easy to replace.

The following are examples of what can be used as objects of reference:

- A paintbrush – art activities
- A wooden spoon – cooking and kitchen
- A pictorial shopping list – shopping
- A picture of a particular shop – kind of shopping
- A trowel – gardening
- A watch, bracelet, key-ring – to represent individual people.

One-to-one work

One-to-one work enables individuals to develop a confidence and tolerance of situations and people. When working one-to-one with a learner, it may be necessary for the facilitator to complete parts of the activity, while encouraging independent participation where possible. There will be occasions when learners will contribute on a passive level only. While there may not be any direct physical participation, experiencing the stages of an activity through sight, touch, smell or sound will encourage and develop an awareness of the immediate environment and people in it.

Working in pairs and small groups

Working in pairs and small groups builds on the foundation of one-to-one work; it encourages an awareness of others, and provides opportunities for interaction.

For a group with a diverse ability range, requiring different levels of assistance, it is possible to designate parts of the activity to individuals or pairs. This will enable each member of the group to make valid contributions at their own pace, with support and encouragement from peers and staff.

Group work

Working in larger groups creates situations that encourage everyone to become involved in an activity in whatever way they can.

Time

The amount of time allocated for each part of an activity will need to be approximate and flexible.

Allow time for

- Locating and setting up equipment
- The unexpected during an activity
- An individual's extended interest in one part of the activity
- Different physical needs of individuals – visual impairment, reduced movement
- Introducing and using new equipment.

Positioning

It is important to consider how and where an individual is positioned during an activity. Being uncomfortable, or unable to see or reach items with ease, may result in a lack of motivation. Allow enough space for the equipment and those who will be using it.

Making adaptations

There will be occasions when adaptations to equipment will need to be made. Some problems may be solved with homemade adaptations, others with manufactured ones, as shown in Table 3.

EXAMPLE PROBLEM	SUGGESTED SOLUTION
How to enable an individual who cannot hold a paintbrush to use one independently.	Make a holder for the paintbrush using a sports wrist support.
How to include an individual with a visual impairment in making a shopping list.	Introduce a different texture for each item on the list. Use the texture with the real item.
How to involve an individual with minimal movement in arms and hands in a group skittles game.	Use a length of plastic drainpipe to drop the ball down to hit the skittles with.

TABLE 3 · **PROBLEMS AND POSSIBLE SOLUTIONS**

Themes

ART & TEXTILES:
Printing

- Cut apple into quarters/halves – print sequences of patterns
- Roll apple across paper to create a pattern, using different colours
- Print on to paper, material or wood
- To explore texture

COOKING:
Baked Apple

- Prepare apple
- Fill apple with dried fruit
- Cook apple
- Explore tastes and textures – apple, raw and cooked; dried fruit – sultanas, sugar, syrup
- Safety and hygiene

Theme

Take an apple

THE ENVIRONMENT:
Growing Plants

- Cut apple in half, look at the position of the seeds
- Remove the seeds
- Fill a flower-pot with compost, plant seeds
- Water seeds
- Observe growth
- Record growth

COMMUNITY LIVING:
Shopping Skills

- Write a shopping list
- Recognise an apple
- Match a picture of an apple to the real object
- Choose an apple
- Use a shopping basket
- Queue and pay for apple
- Put apple into shopping bag

WORKSHEET 1

THEME: TAKE AN APPLE
Art & Textiles – Printing

FOCUS OBJECTIVES

- To encourage self-expression
- To develop spatial awareness
- To develop sequencing skills
- To encourage exploration of the texture of art materials and equipment
- To develop colour recognition and matching

EQUIPMENT

Apples
Knife and chopping board
Paper, plain material, card, wood
Selection of ready-mix paint
PVA glue
Paint trays – one for each colour
Paintbrushes – one for each group member
Overalls – one for each group member
Newspaper – to cover tables

METHOD

Printing

1. Explore the texture of the apples by holding and feeling them.
2. Cut apples into halves and quarters – feel the difference between the skin and the flesh inside the apple.
3. Pour paints into trays – mix in a small amount of PVA glue to prevent paint flaking when dry.
4. Feel the paper, card, material, wood, etc, and select a surface to make a print on.
5. Apply the paint to the apple segments using the paintbrushes.
6. Press apple segments firmly on to chosen surface.
7. Gently lift off apple – or peel the paper or material off the apple.
8. Build up a symmetrical pattern.

Rolling

1. Coat the whole apple with paint, either by rolling it in the paint tray or by using a paintbrush.
2. Secure the paper or material to the table using masking tape.
3. Gently roll one apple across the paper.
4. Repeat with different apples and colours to create a random pattern.
5. Try mono-prints – focus on one colour.

Speechmark  This page may be photocopied for instructional use only. *Themed Activities for People with Learning Difficulties* © M Hutchinson 2003

RECORDING SHEET 1

THEME: TAKE AN APPLE
Art & Textiles – Printing

Name: ______________________ Date: ______________________

FOCUS OBJECTIVES	OBSERVATIONS AND COMMENTS
To encourage self-expression	
To develop spatial awareness	
To develop sequencing skills	
To encourage exploration of the texture of art materials and equipment	
To develop colour recognition and matching	

This page may be photocopied for instructional use only. *Themed Activities for People with Learning Difficulties* © M Hutchinson 2003

Speechmark

WORKSHEET 2

THEME: TAKE AN APPLE
Cooking – Baked Apple

FOCUS OBJECTIVES

- To extend experiences of taste and smell
- To develop hand-eye coordination
- To develop sequencing skills
- To develop an awareness of safety and hygiene

EQUIPMENT

4 large cooking apples
50 g/2 oz currants or sultanas
25 g/1 oz soft brown sugar
4 teaspoons golden syrup
25 g/1 oz butter or margarine
Margarine to grease oven-proof dish
Teaspoons – one for each group member
Apple corer, chopping board and oven-proof dish
Aprons – one for each group member

METHOD

Baking

1 Heat oven to 180 °C, 350 °F, gas 4.
2 Wash and core apples – recycle cores by putting them in a compost bin.
3 Place apples in a greased oven-proof dish.
4 Fill centre of each apple with the fruit and sugar mixed together – push down with a teaspoon.
5 Pour a teaspoon of syrup over each apple.
6 Add a small knob of butter to the top of each apple.
7 Sprinkle a little sugar over apples.
8 Bake in the oven for 40–50 minutes.

Safety and Hygiene

1 Wash hands before activity.
2 Wear aprons to protect clothing.
3 Talk about how to use sharp knives.
4 Discuss why oven-gloves should always be used when baking.
5 Keep surfaces and utensils clean.

Speechmark This page may be photocopied for instructional use only. *Themed Activities for People with Learning Difficulties* © M Hutchinson 2003

RECORDING SHEET 2

THEME: TAKE AN APPLE
Cooking – Baked Apple

Name: ____________________ Date: ____________________

FOCUS OBJECTIVES	OBSERVATIONS AND COMMENTS
To extend experiences of taste	
To extend experiences of smell	
To develop hand-eye coordination	
To develop sequencing skills	
To develop an awareness of safety and hygiene	

This page may be photocopied for instructional use only. *Themed Activities for People with Learning Difficulties* © M Hutchinson 2003

Speechmark

WORKSHEET 3

THEME: TAKE AN APPLE

The Environment – Growing Plants

FOCUS OBJECTIVES

- To encourage observation skills
- To develop exploratory techniques
- To develop sequencing skills
- To encourage participation in group projects
- To develop fine motor skills

EQUIPMENT

Apples – one for each pair of group members
Knife and chopping board
Pen, coloured paper, ruler
Newspaper – to cover tables
Gardening aprons – one for each group member
Flowerpots – one for each group member
Compost
Trowels – to share
Watering can

METHOD

Planting

1. Cut apples into halves.
2. Give half an apple to each person in the group.
3. Locate the seeds in the apple.
4. Remove the seeds from the apple.
5. Fill a flowerpot with compost, 2cm ($^3/_4$in) from the top.
6. Gently place seeds into the compost.
7. Cover seeds with compost, and water.

Recording Growth

1. Make a bar graph – use individuals' names linked with a chosen colour.
2. Measure growth of seedlings on a daily/weekly basis.
3. Cut coloured paper to appropriate lengths and glue on to the bar graph.
4. Buy seedlings from a local garden centre, if the seeds do not grow.

This page may be photocopied for instructional use only. *Themed Activities for People with Learning Difficulties* © M Hutchinson 2003

RECORDING SHEET 3

THEME: TAKE AN APPLE
The Environment – Growing Plants

Name: ______________________ Date: ______________________

FOCUS OBJECTIVES	OBSERVATIONS AND COMMENTS
To encourage observation skills	
To develop exploratory techniques	
To develop sequencing skills	
To encourage participation in group projects	
To develop fine motor skills	

This page may be photocopied for instructional use only. *Themed Activities for People with Learning Difficulties* © M Hutchinson 2003

WORKSHEET 4

THEME: TAKE AN APPLE
Community Living – Shopping Skills

FOCUS OBJECTIVES

- To have opportunities to make choices
- To develop matching skills
- To develop confidence in a variety of community-based settings
- To develop waiting skills
- To work on literacy and numeracy skills

EQUIPMENT

Pen and paper
Purse/wallet with money
Shopping bag
Transport
Photographs/pictures of apples

METHOD

Preparation for Trip

1 Write the list using written, pictorial and symbolic forms.
2 Count out money and place into purse or wallet.
3 Look at pictures of shops and select a picture of a supermarket, greengrocer's or market stall.
4 Choose where to buy the apples.
5 Talk about the journey to the shop.

Buying the Apples

1 Find a shopping basket and look at the shopping list.
2 Walk around the shop and locate the fruit section.
3 Refer to the shopping list and match a picture of an apple to a real one.
4 Choose what kind of apple, or selection of apples, to buy.
5 Go to a checkout and transfer the apples from the basket to the conveyor belt.
6 Pay for the apples – hand over the money and wait for the receipt and any change.
7 Put apples into shopping bag.

Speechmark P This page may be photocopied for instructional use only. *Themed Activities for People with Learning Difficulties* © M Hutchinson 2003

RECORDING SHEET 4

THEME: TAKE AN APPLE
Community Living – Shopping Skills

Name: __________ Date: __________

FOCUS OBJECTIVES	OBSERVATIONS AND COMMENTS
To have opportunities to make choices	
To develop matching skills	
To develop confidence in a variety of community-based settings	
To develop waiting skills	
To work on literacy and numeracy skills	

This page may be photocopied for instructional use only. *Themed Activities for People with Learning Difficulties* © M Hutchinson 2003 Speechmark

SELF-EXPRESSION:
Picture Essay

- Choose a topic
- Research the topic
- Take photographs to illustrate the topic
- Develop and print film
- Select photographs
- Decide a sequence for photographs
- Present picture essay

DESIGN & TECHNOLOGY:
Portrait Dominoes

- Cut plywood into 8cm x 10cm (3in x 4in) rectangles
- Sand edges
- Take portrait photographs of people
- Trim photographs and glue on to plywood
- Varnish dominoes

Theme

Take a camera

THE ENVIRONMENT:
Map of Local Shops

- Make a list of shops in the street
- Take photographs of each shop
- Make a pictorial map of the shops using the photographs
- Take photographs of what each shop sells

ICT SKILLS:
Using a Camera

- Load/unload film into a camera
- Operate the camera
- Discuss composition of photograph
- Take film to be developed and printed
- Mount photographs

WORKSHEET 1

THEME: TAKE A CAMERA
Self-Expression – Picture Essay

FOCUS OBJECTIVES

- To develop choice and decision-making
- To encourage self-expression
- To develop sequencing skills
- To develop research techniques
- To develop fine motor skills

EQUIPMENT

Access to local environment, library, books and magazines
Camera – any kind
Films – colour or black and white
Folder to keep photographs in
Paper/card for display
PVA glue/glue stick
Guillotine/craft knife and cutting board
Photograph album

METHOD

Research for picture essay

1. Choose a topic – eg, types of houses, transport, clothes, friends, families.
2. Gather information about the topic – from magazines, books, library, etc.
3. Take photographs about the topic – try black and white and/or colour films.
4. Get the film developed and printed.
5. Keep all information gathered in a folder.

Creating a picture essay

1. Decide how many photographs will make up the picture essay.
2. Select photographs and choose a sequence or pattern to present them in – use either colour or black and white, the essay will be more dramatic if one type of film is used.
3. Glue the photographs on to backing paper, and cut a thin border around each picture.
4. Attach mounted photographs to display card, or secure in a photograph album in the chosen sequence.
5. Add a label with a title and name on it.

 Speechmark  This page may be photocopied for instructional use only. *Themed Activities for People with Learning Difficulties* © M Hutchinson 2003

RECORDING SHEET 1

THEME: TAKE A CAMERA
Self-Expression – Picture Essay

Name: ______________________ Date: ______________

FOCUS OBJECTIVES	OBSERVATIONS AND COMMENTS
To develop choice and decision-making	
To encourage self-expression	
To develop sequencing skills	
To develop research techniques	
To develop fine motor skills	

This page may be photocopied for instructional use only. *Themed Activities for People with Learning Difficulties* © M Hutchinson 2003

WORKSHEET 2

THEME: TAKE A CAMERA
Design & Technology – Portrait Dominoes

FOCUS OBJECTIVES

- To develop awareness of self and others
- To encourage choice and decision-making
- To develop hand-eye coordination
- To develop matching skills
- To encourage participation in group activities

EQUIPMENT

Plywood/hardboard
Small saw
Sandpaper
Camera and film
Scissors or craft knife and cutting board
PVA glue/glue stick
Clear varnish and paintbrush

METHOD

Preparation for Dominoes

1 Decide how many pairs of dominoes are needed.
2 Take portrait photographs – head and shoulders only – of each member of the group.
3 Have two sets of photographs developed and printed.

Making the Dominoes

1 On a piece of plywood or hardboard, mark out 8cm x 10cm (3in x 4in) rectangles – one for each photograph.
2 Cut out the rectangles.
3 Sand the edges of each rectangle.
4 Select each pair of photographs to be used and trim to the size of the dominoes.
5 Glue each photograph on to a domino.
6 Coat each domino, portrait side up, with clear varnish.
7 When dry, turn the dominoes over and glue on a name label.
8 Varnish this side of each domino and leave to dry.

Speechmark P This page may be photocopied for instructional use only. *Themed Activities for People with Learning Difficulties* © M Hutchinson 2003

RECORDING SHEET 2

THEME: TAKE A CAMERA
Design & Technology – Portrait Dominoes

Name:

Date:

FOCUS OBJECTIVES	OBSERVATIONS AND COMMENTS
To develop awareness of self and others	
To encourage choice and decision-making	
To develop hand-eye coordination	
To develop matching skills	
To encourage participation in group activities	

This page may be photocopied for instructional use only. *Themed Activities for People with Learning Difficulties* © M Hutchinson 2003

WORKSHEET 3

THEME: TAKE A CAMERA
The Environment – Map of Local Shops

FOCUS OBJECTIVES

- To encourage observation skills
- To develop matching skills
- To develop sequencing skills
- To encourage participation in group projects
- To develop environmental awareness

EQUIPMENT

Notepad and pen
Camera and film
2–3 large sheets of card
Scissors
PVA glue/glue stick
Self-adhesive labels
Folder to keep work in

METHOD

Preparation

1 Walk along area of local shops.
2 Make a list of each shop – its name and what it sells.
3 Take photographs of the front of each shop.
4 Take photographs of what each shop sells – check with the manager before taking photographs inside the shop.
5 Have the film developed and printed.

Making the Map

1 Position the photographs on to the large sheets of card, in the same order as the shops.
2 Glue the photographs to the card.
3 Label each photograph with the name of the shop and what kind of shop it is – use the self-adhesive labels for this.
4 Make a title for the pictorial map, and glue it above the photographs.
5 Display for others to refer to.
6 Extend the project by laminating copies of each photograph used in the map, to provide a selection of cards from which to choose which shops to use during an outing.

Speechmark P This page may be photocopied for instructional use only. *Themed Activities for People with Learning Difficulties* © M Hutchinson 2003

RECORDING SHEET 3

THEME: TAKE A CAMERA
The Environment – Map of Local Shops

Name: ______________________ Date: ______________________

FOCUS OBJECTIVES	OBSERVATIONS AND COMMENTS
To encourage observation skills	
To develop matching skills	
To develop sequencing skills	
To encourage participation in group projects	
To develop environmental awareness	

This page may be photocopied for instructional use only. *Themed Activities for People with Learning Difficulties* © M Hutchinson 2003

WORKSHEET 4

THEME: TAKE A CAMERA
ICT Skills – Using a Camera

FOCUS OBJECTIVES

- To develop fine motor skills
- To have opportunities to make choices through discussion
- To encourage self-expression
- To develop an understanding of cause and effect
- To develop waiting skills

EQUIPMENT

35mm camera and 100 ASA colour film/disposable camera
Book about the basics of photography
Selection of magazines
Thin card, paper
Scissors
Glue
Folder to keep work in
Mounting card

METHOD

Looking at and Using a Camera

1. Use the book to find out about the camera.
2. Draw a simple outline of a camera, and label it.
3. Pick up the camera – feel the shape and weight of it.
4. Look through the viewfinder and practise pressing the trigger.
5. Open the camera and load the film.
6. Make a written and/or illustrated list of ideas to photograph, use pictures from magazines to represent different subjects.
7. Choose ideas from the examples of people, places or objects.
8. Take several photographs of each subject chosen.
9. When the film is finished, rewind it (if not automatic) and remove from the camera.
10. Have the film developed and printed.
11. Select one or more photographs and mount on to card ready to display.

This page may be photocopied for instructional use only. *Themed Activities for People with Learning Difficulties* © M Hutchinson 2003

Speechmark

RECORDING SHEET 4

THEME: TAKE A CAMERA
ICT Skills – Using a Camera

Name: ______________________ Date: ______________

FOCUS OBJECTIVES	OBSERVATIONS AND COMMENTS
To develop fine motor skills	
To have opportunities to make choice through discussion	
To encourage self-expression	
To develop an understanding of cause and effect	
To develop waiting skills	

This page may be photocopied for instructional use only. *Themed Activities for People with Learning Difficulties* © M Hutchinson 2003

ART & TEXTILES:
Bead Mobile

- Cut shell in half and remove coconut flesh
- Thread beads on to nylon thread or lightweight fishing line
- Attach strings of beads to coconut shell
- Varnish or paint shell
- Suspend mobile from ceiling

THE ENVIRONMENT:
Bird Feeder

- Use the coconut shell to make a birdfeeder
- Buy seeds
- Buy nuts and lard
- Mix together ingredients
- Fill empty half of coconut shell with mixture
- Hang birdfeeder in garden

Theme

Take a coconut

COOKING:
Vegetable Curry

- Cut coconut in half
- Scoop out the fresh coconut
- Wash and chop vegetables
- Cook vegetables and coconut with curry sauce
- Sprinkle curry with grated coconut and serve with rice

COMMUNICATION:
Interactive Games

- Use coconuts to make a coconut shy and set of skittles
- Drain milk out of coconuts and paint shells in bright colours
- Make containers to hold coconuts – for coconut shy
- Join in team games

WORKSHEET 1

THEME: TAKE A COCONUT
Art & Textiles – Bead Mobile

FOCUS OBJECTIVES

- To encourage tactile and visual exploration
- To develop fine motor skills
- To develop sequencing skills
- To encourage exploration of art materials and equipment
- To develop colour recognition and matching

EQUIPMENT

1 coconut
Saw
Knife
Nylon thread or lightweight fishing line
Selection of large beads
Drill or awl
Varnish and/or paint
Paintbrush
9 large buttons

METHOD

1. Saw the coconut in half horizontally and remove the flesh.
2. Take one half of the coconut and drill four small holes about 2.5 cm (1 in) in from the edge, and equal distances apart, and one small hole in the centre of the coconut.
3. Cut four lengths of nylon thread, each about 35 cm (12 in) long.
4. Tie a button on to one end of each length of thread – to keep the beads on the thread.
5. Decide on a sequence for the beads – colour, size, etc – and thread the beads on to each length of thread.
6. Take the excess thread left at the top of one string of beads and feed through one of the holes around the edge of the coconut shell.
7. Add one of the buttons to the thread and tie securely.
8. Repeat the process for the remaining strings of beads.
9. Use a length of thread, the ninth button and the central hole, to make a loop to hang the mobile from.
10. Trim any excess thread from the bottom of each string of beads.

Speechmark  This page may be photocopied for instructional use only. *Themed Activities for People with Learning Difficulties* © M Hutchinson 2003

RECORDING SHEET 1

THEME: TAKE A COCONUT
Art & Textiles – Bead Mobile

Name: __________ Date: __________

FOCUS OBJECTIVES	OBSERVATIONS AND COMMENTS
To encourage tactile and visual exploration	
To develop fine motor skills	
To develop sequencing skills	
To encourage exploration of art materials and equipment	
To develop colour recognition and matching	

This page may be photocopied for instructional use only. *Themed Activities for People with Learning Difficulties* © M Hutchinson 2003

WORKSHEET 2

THEME: TAKE A COCONUT
The Environment – Bird Feeder

FOCUS OBJECTIVES

- To encourage an awareness of the environment
- To develop fine motor skills
- To develop sequencing skills
- To encourage exploration of different textures
- To develop an understanding of cause and effect

EQUIPMENT

1 coconut
Saw
Drill
Large saucepan and tablespoon
Lard – 225 g (½ lb)
Bag of wild bird seed/peanuts
String
2 flowerpots

METHOD

1. Saw coconut in half and remove flesh.
2. Drill two holes into the centre of each coconut half.
3. Thread a short length of string through both holes, and tie the ends together to make a loop.
4. Fill one empty coconut shell with the birdseed.
5. Melt the lard in the saucepan and remove from the cooker.
6. Tip the seed from the coconut shell into the saucepan and mix well.
7. Allow the mixture to cool to a soft consistency, but not to set.
8. Spoon the soft mixture into each coconut shell.
9. Stand each coconut shell on a flowerpot while the mixture sets.
10. When the mixture has set, tip the coconut shells upside down and use the string loops to hang in the garden.
11. Use the bird feeder during cold weather, when natural food supplies are scarce.

This page may be photocopied for instructional use only. *Themed Activities for People with Learning Difficulties* © M Hutchinson 2003

RECORDING SHEET 2

THEME: TAKE A COCONUT
The Environment – Bird Feeder

Name: ______________________ Date: ______________________

FOCUS OBJECTIVES	OBSERVATIONS AND COMMENTS
To encourage an awareness of the environment	
To develop fine motor skills	
To develop sequencing skills	
To encourage exploration of different textures	
To develop an understanding of cause and effect	

This page may be photocopied for instructional use only. *Themed Activities for People with Learning Difficulties* © M Hutchinson 2003

WORKSHEET 3

THEME: TAKE A COCONUT
Cooking – Vegetable Curry

FOCUS OBJECTIVES

- To extend experiences of taste and smell
- To develop sequencing skills
- To explore colour and shape
- To develop an awareness of safety and hygiene
- To develop fine motor skills

EQUIPMENT

Saucepan
Chopping board and knife
1 coconut
4 hard-boiled eggs
2 large onions
120 ml/4 fl oz cooking oil
1 teaspoon chilli powder, 1 tablespoon ground coriander
2 teaspoons cumin powder, 1 teaspoon salt
1 lemon
Serving dish
Aprons – for each group member

METHOD

Cooking

1. Open coconut, remove the flesh and cut it into thin slices.
2. Squeeze lemon juice over the coconut flesh.
3. Peel, chop and fry the onions in the cooking oil.
4. When the onions are soft, stir in the chilli powder, coriander, cumin and salt.
5. Add the coconut flesh and 300 ml ($\frac{1}{2}$ pint) of water, and simmer for 10–15 minutes.
6. Remove the shells from the hard-boiled eggs, and cut the eggs into wedges.
7. Arrange the eggs in a serving dish and pour the coconut curry sauce over them.

Safety and Hygiene

1. Wash hands before the activity.
2. Wear aprons to protect clothing.
3. Talk about how to use sharp knives.
4. Discuss how to position a saucepan safely on a cooker.
5. Keep surfaces and utensils clean.

Speechmark P This page may be photocopied for instructional use only. *Themed Activities for People with Learning Difficulties* © M Hutchinson 2003

RECORDING SHEET 3

THEME: TAKE A COCONUT
Cooking – Vegetable Curry

Name: ______________________ Date: ______________________

FOCUS OBJECTIVES	OBSERVATIONS AND COMMENTS
To extend experience of taste and smell	
To develop sequencing skills	
To explore colour and shape	
To develop an awareness of safety and hygiene	
To develop fine motor skills	

This page may be photocopied for instructional use only. *Themed Activities for People with Learning Difficulties* © M Hutchinson 2003

WORKSHEET 4

THEME: TAKE A COCONUT
Communication – Interactive Games

FOCUS OBJECTIVES

- To develop hand-eye coordination
- To develop colour recognition
- To encourage participation in group activities
- To develop turn-taking skills
- To develop an awareness of others

EQUIPMENT

6 coconuts
Wood file
3 different colours of paint
PVA glue or varnish
Paintbrushes
Newspaper
Overalls
Small heavy ball or soft small ball

METHOD

Making the Skittles

1. Check that each coconut will stand up without falling over.
2. Level the bottom of any coconut if required, using the wood file.
3. Paint the coconuts – 2 of each colour. Do not paint the bottom of the coconuts.
4. Leave the coconuts to dry, by standing them on sheets of newspaper.
5. Paint numbers on to the coconut skittles – optional.

To Play

1. Position coconut skittles in a triangular shape, semi-circle or straight line.
2. Use a small heavy ball when skittles are positioned on the floor, or a softer ball if played as table skittles.
3. Take turns to either knock down all the skittles, aim for one colour, or a particular number.
4. Play as a team game and keep score.

Speechmark P This page may be photocopied for instructional use only. *Themed Activities for People with Learning Difficulties* © M Hutchinson 2003

RECORDING SHEET 4

THEME: TAKE A COCONUT
Communication – Interactive Games

Name: Date:

FOCUS OBJECTIVES	OBSERVATIONS AND COMMENTS
To develop hand-eye coordination	
To develop colour recognition	
To encourage participation in group activities	
To develop turn-taking skills	
To develop an awareness of others	

This page may be photocopied for instructional use only. *Themed Activities for People with Learning Difficulties* © M Hutchinson 2003

DRAMA:
Poem or Story

- Choose and adapt narrative
- Make props – eg, length of material to represent sea/river/sail/cave
- Make costumes
- Use material as a stage curtain
- Practise and perform adapted outline

COMMUNICATION:
Interactive Games

- Mini-parachute game
- Pass items along a length of material – linear or circular
- Wrap mystery objects in a piece of material; feel and guess item
- Guess who? Who is behind the material?

Theme

Take a piece of material

ART & TEXTILES:
Soft Sculpture

- Select a base piece of material for the sculpture – look at length, colour and texture
- Cut strips of material to add to the sculpture
- Position and attach strips of material to base material

COMMUNITY LIVING:
Household Skills

- Wash up dirty crockery
- Use a tea-towel to dry clean crockery
- Put away dry crockery
- Place used tea-towel in linen basket
- Wash dirty linen
- Dry and put away clean tea-towel

WORKSHEET 1

THEME: TAKE A PIECE OF MATERIAL
Drama – Poem or Story

FOCUS OBJECTIVES

- To have opportunities to make choices
- To encourage self-expression
- To encourage turn-taking and waiting skills
- To develop self-confidence and assertiveness
- To work on literacy skills

EQUIPMENT

Length of material – eg, an old sheet
Books of poems or traditional stories
Costumes – cloaks, shawls, hats, etc – if required
Scissors
PVA glue/glue sticks
Cardboard
Paint

METHOD

Preparation

1 Choose a poem or story, or write one.
2 Adapt the narrative where necessary – for example, focus on the theme of a poem/story, reduce or extend the length, etc.
3 List characters, backgrounds, props and costumes needed.
4 Make props and costumes – keep them simple.
5 Use a plain sheet to paint the backdrop on.
6 Incorporate material in the costumes and props.
7 Allocate jobs and roles to all group members.

Performance

1 Suspend backdrop.
2 If needed, make a stage curtain from a piece of material.
3 Have a 'rehearsal', using the stage area and the props.
4 Invite guests to be the audience.
5 Video the performance.

Speechmark P This page may be photocopied for instructional use only. *Themed Activities for People with Learning Difficulties* © M Hutchinson 2003

RECORDING SHEET 1

THEME: TAKE A PIECE OF MATERIAL
Drama – Poem or Story

Name: ____________________ Date: ____________________

FOCUS OBJECTIVES	OBSERVATIONS AND COMMENTS
To have opportunities to make choices	
To encourage self-expression	
To encourage turn-taking and waiting skills	
To develop self-confidence and assertiveness	
To work on literacy skills	

This page may be photocopied for instructional use only. *Themed Activities for People with Learning Difficulties* © M Hutchinson 2003

WORKSHEET 2

THEME: TAKE A PIECE OF MATERIAL
Communication – Interactive Games

FOCUS OBJECTIVES

- To encourage participation in group activities
- To develop eye contact
- To develop listening skills
- To develop turn-taking skills
- To encourage tactile exploration

EQUIPMENT

Material – long strip/large square or circle
Variety or objects – for example, a belt, hoop, necklace, T-shirt, watch, alarm clock, auditory ball, plastic cup, hat, etc
Box to keep objects in
Range of music – quiet and slow/loud and fast
Cassette player

METHOD

Mini-Parachute Game

1 Stand or sit in a circle.
2 Use a large square or circle of material as the mini-parachute; move it up and down with a gentle motion.
3 Gradually increase speed, then reduce it.
4 Introduce music – move the parachute to the rhythm of the music.

Passing Game

1 Sit in a circle or line.
2 Pass a strip of material around the group, and encourage individuals to hold or touch it.
3 Thread an object – for example, a belt, hoop, T-shirt, etc, on to the strip of material, and pass it along the length of material around the group.
4 Repeat with a selection of objects.

Mystery Objects

1 Wrap a mystery object in a piece of material.
2 Feel and guess the object – repeat with different objects.

Guess Who?

1 Suspend or hold up a piece of material.
2 Choose someone to stand behind the material.
3 Ask questions to guess who it is.

Speechmark P This page may be photocopied for instructional use only. *Themed Activities for People with Learning Difficulties* © M Hutchinson 2003

RECORDING SHEET 2

THEME: TAKE A PIECE OF MATERIAL
Communication – Interactive Games

Name: ______________________ Date: ______________________

FOCUS OBJECTIVES	OBSERVATIONS AND COMMENTS
To encourage participation in group activities	
To develop eye contact	
To develop listening skills	
To develop turn-taking skills	
To encourage tactile exploration	

This page may be photocopied for instructional use only. *Themed Activities for People with Learning Difficulties* © M Hutchinson 2003

WORKSHEET 3 | THEME: TAKE A PIECE OF MATERIAL

Art & Textiles – Soft Sculpture

FOCUS OBJECTIVES

- To develop tactile exploration
- To develop visual tracking
- To develop sequencing skills
- To encourage working in pairs
- To provide opportunities for making choices

EQUIPMENT

Large piece of plain material or netting
Selection of ribbon, strips of coloured and patterned material
Strips of crêpe paper, string, wool, bubblewrap, etc
Scissors

METHOD

1. Suspend the large piece of plain material or netting from the ceiling – low enough for someone sitting down to reach.
2. If using material, make numerous small cuts in it at random distances apart.
3. Have a selection of ribbon, strips of material, crêpe paper, etc on a table near the material.
4. Encourage individuals to choose an item from the table, or from two items offered, through eye-contact or vocalisation.
5. Feed one end of the ribbon or strip of material through one of the small cuts in the material, or through the holes in the netting.
6. Pull the ribbon or strip of material half way through the cut or hole.
7. Select another cut in the material or hole in the netting – not too far away from the original one – feed one end of the ribbon or strip of material back through it.
8. Tie the two ends of the ribbon or strip of material together – they should be on the same side of the large piece of material or netting.
9. Continue to add items to build up a colourful and textured banner.
10. To encourage working as a pair, position individuals on either side of a piece of netting. The movements of each person, and choice of materials added, can be watched through the netting.

Speechmark P This page may be photocopied for instructional use only. *Themed Activities for People with Learning Difficulties* © M Hutchinson 2003

RECORDING SHEET 3

THEME: TAKE A PIECE OF MATERIAL
Art & Textiles – Soft Sculpture

Name: ______________________ Date: ______________________

FOCUS OBJECTIVES	OBSERVATIONS AND COMMENTS
To develop tactile exploration	
To develop visual tracking	
To develop sequencing skills	
To encourage working in pairs	
To provide opportunities for making choices	

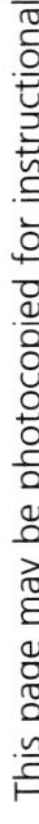
This page may be photocopied for instructional use only. *Themed Activities for People with Learning Difficulties* © M Hutchinson 2003

WORKSHEET 4

THEME: TAKE A PIECE OF MATERIAL
Community Living – Household Skills

FOCUS OBJECTIVES

- To develop an understanding of clean and dirty
- To develop matching skills
- To encourage participation in routines
- To develop an understanding of cause and effect
- To encourage passing skills

EQUIPMENT

Sink or washing-up bowl
Dirty crockery
Tea-towel
Washing machine
Dryer or airer
Washing-up liquid and detergent

METHOD

1. Fill the sink or washing up bowl with hand-hot water.
2. Add the washing-up liquid.
3. Place the dirty crockery into the sink or washing-up bowl.
4. Wash the crockery and place on draining board.
5. Use a clean tea-towel to dry the crockery.
6. Put away the clean and dry crockery.
7. Place the used tea-towel in the linen basket.
8. Transfer the dirty linen to the washing machine.
9. Add the washing detergent.
10. Select the correct washing cycle and switch on machine.
11. After cycle has finished, remove the wet washing and place in the dryer or on the airer.
12. Put away the clean and dry tea-towel.

Speechmark  This page may be photocopied for instructional use only. *Themed Activities for People with Learning Difficulties* © M Hutchinson 2003

RECORDING SHEET 4

THEME: TAKE A PIECE OF MATERIAL
Community Living – Household Skills

Name: ______________________ Date: ______________________

FOCUS OBJECTIVES	OBSERVATIONS AND COMMENTS
To develop an understanding of clean and dirty	
To develop matching skills	
To encourage participation in routines	
To develop an understanding of cause and effect	
To encourage passing skills	

 This page may be photocopied for instructional use only. *Themed Activities for People with Learning Difficulties* © M Hutchinson 2003

THE ENVIRONMENT:
Miniature Rockery

- Collect a variety of small stones
- Wash and dry stones
- Fill a small container with compost
- Add small rockery plants
- Position stones among the plants
- Water plants

ART & TEXTILES:
Painting

- Select a flat-surfaced stone
- Choose a design – original, Celtic, Aboriginal, African, Indian, etc
- Draw design on to stone
- Paint and varnish design

Theme

Take a stone

SCIENCE & TECHNOLOGY:
Measuring and Weighing

- Select different sized stones
- Draw around each stone and measure diameter
- Weigh each stone
- Make a size and weight chart with the information

COMMUNICATION:
Interactive Games

- Pass the Stone – team game using one stone and a blanket
- Noughts and Crosses – paint noughts and crosses on to stones
- How Many in the Bag? – place a number of stones in a bag for teams to feel and guess

WORKSHEET 1

THEME: TAKE A STONE
The Environment – Miniature Rockery

FOCUS OBJECTIVES

- To encourage tactile exploration
- To develop spatial awareness
- To develop colour recognition and matching
- To develop sequencing skills
- To provide opportunities for making choices

EQUIPMENT

Selection of small stones
Bowl and cloth
Newspaper – to cover tables
Small container – flowerpot, bowl, etc
Compost and trowel, or old tablespoon
Small rockery plants – 2 or 3, depending on size of container

METHOD

Making a Rockery

1. Fill the bowl with hand-hot water.
2. Wash the stones.
3. Dry the stones with the cloth.
4. Cover the table with newspaper.
5. Fill the small container with compost, using the trowel or spoon – do not fill the container completely full.
6. Use the handle of the trowel or spoon as a dibber to make a small hole in the compost.
7. Gently place a rockery plant in the hole.
8. Fill any gaps around the base of the plant with compost to secure the plant.
9. Repeat with the other rockery plants.
10. Choose 2–3 stones and position them around the plants.
11. Water the plants.

This page may be photocopied for instructional use only. *Themed Activities for People with Learning Difficulties* © M Hutchinson 2003

Speechmark

RECORDING SHEET 1

THEME: TAKE A STONE
The Environment – Miniature Rockery

Name: ____________________ Date: ____________________

FOCUS OBJECTIVES	OBSERVATIONS AND COMMENTS
To encourage tactile exploration	
To develop spatial awareness	
To develop colour recognition and matching	
To develop sequencing skills	
To provide opportunities for making choices	

This page may be photocopied for instructional use only. *Themed Activities for People with Learning Difficulties* © M Hutchinson 2003

Speechmark

WORKSHEET 2

THEME: TAKE A STONE
Art & Textiles – Painting

FOCUS OBJECTIVES

- To encourage self-expression
- To develop spatial awareness
- To develop choice-making skills
- To develop research skills
- To encourage tactile exploration

EQUIPMENT

Aprons – one for each group member
Newspaper – to cover tables
Selection of ready-mix paint
PVA glue
Varnish
Paint trays and brushes
Flat-surfaced stones
Books with ideas for designs – Celtic, Aboriginal, etc
Plain paper and a pencil

METHOD

Painting designs

1. Wash and dry the stones.
2. For each stone, select the surface to be painted.
3. Look through a selection of designs for ideas.
4. Use a design from one of the books, or make one up.
5. Copy the design on to the stone.
6. The design can be drawn on to the stone first using a pencil, and then painted.
7. It can also be painted directly on to the stone using a brush.
8. Select one or more colours to paint the design with.
9. Mix a small amount of PVA glue into the paint to stop it flaking off the stone.
10. Allow the paint to dry.
11. Varnish the painted side of the stone and allow to dry.

Speechmark P This page may be photocopied for instructional use only. *Themed Activities for People with Learning Difficulties* © M Hutchinson 2003

RECORDING SHEET 2

THEME: TAKE A STONE
Art & Textiles – Painting

Name: ______________________ Date: ______________

FOCUS OBJECTIVES	OBSERVATIONS AND COMMENTS
To encourage self-expression	
To develop spatial awareness	
To develop choice-making skills	
To develop research skills	
To encourage tactile exploration	

This page may be photocopied for instructional use only. *Themed Activities for People with Learning Difficulties* © M Hutchinson 2003

WORKSHEET 3

THEME: TAKE A STONE
Science & Technology – Measuring and Weighing

FOCUS OBJECTIVES

- To encourage observation skills
- To develop an understanding of big, small, heavy and light
- To develop numeracy skills
- To encourage participation in group projects
- To develop fine motor skills

EQUIPMENT

6 different-sized stones
Kitchen scales
Ruler
Sheets of paper – 6 different colours
Pencil
Scissors
Large sheet of paper
Glue stick

METHOD

Looking at Size and Weight

1. Count how many stones there are.
2. Place each stone on a different-coloured piece of paper.
3. Draw around each stone on pieces of paper.
4. Cut out each stone shape and number from 1 to 6.
5. Measure the diameter of each stone shape and write the information on each.
6. Pair each stone with its paper stone shape.
7. Weigh each stone on the kitchen scales, and again record the information on each stone shape.
8. Position the paper stones on the large sheet of paper in size order – largest on the left, smallest on the right.
9. Secure each shape with the glue stick.
10. Label the chart *Looking at Size and Weight.*

 This page may be photocopied for instructional use only. *Themed Activities for People with Learning Difficulties* © M Hutchinson 2003 Speechmark

RECORDING SHEET 3

THEME: TAKE A STONE
Science & Technology – Measuring and Weighing

Name: ____________________ Date: ____________________

FOCUS OBJECTIVES	OBSERVATIONS AND COMMENTS
To encourage observation skills	
To develop an understanding of big, small, heavy and light	
To develop numeracy skills	
To encourage participation in group projects	
To develop fine motor skills	

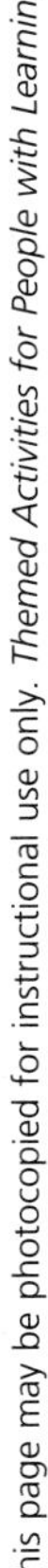
This page may be photocopied for instructional use only. *Themed Activities for People with Learning Difficulties* © M Hutchinson 2003

Speechmark

WORKSHEET 4

THEME: TAKE A STONE
Communication – Interactive Games

FOCUS OBJECTIVES

- To have opportunities to make choices
- To develop passing skills
- To develop turn-taking skills
- To encourage working as part of a team
- To develop numeracy skills

EQUIPMENT

1 small stone
A blanket or table-cloth
10 medium-sized stones
Cloth bag

METHOD

Pass the Stone

1. Divide the group into two equal teams.
2. Sit teams opposite each other across a table.
3. Decide which team is to pass the stone first, and cover their hands with the blanket or table-cloth.
4. Put the stone into the hand of one member of the team with the blanket.
5. On the word 'go', the stone is passed among the team members.
6. The other team watch while the stone is shuffled between people.
7. After 30–40 seconds, the team with the stone stop passing it between themselves. With one person holding it, they keep their hands under the blanket.
8. The team watching then have to guess who is holding the stone.
9. Give the blanket and stone to the team who watched and play again.

How Many in the Bag?

1. Put a random number of stones in a cloth bag.
2. Pass the bag around the group.
3. Encourage individuals to feel the bag and guess how many stones are in it.
4. Write down each person's guess.
5. Tip the stones out of the bag and count them.
6. Repeat with different numbers of stones in the bag.

Speechmark P This page may be photocopied for instructional use only. *Themed Activities for People with Learning Difficulties* © M Hutchinson 2003

RECORDING SHEET 4

THEME: TAKE A STONE
Communication – Interactive Games

Name: ______________________ Date: ______________________

FOCUS OBJECTIVES	OBSERVATIONS AND COMMENTS
To have opportunities to make choices	
To develop passing skills	
To develop turn-taking skills	
To encourage working as part of a team	
To develop numeracy skills	

This page may be photocopied for instructional use only. *Themed Activities for People with Learning Difficulties* © M Hutchinson 2003

Speechmark

DRAMA:
Shadow Screen

- Choose a theme to build on – eg, Chinese New Year, Christmas
- Explore moving images – move objects across overhead projector surface, body movements, ribbon-stick, branch, moving screen – link to story
- Make props and music

THE ENVIRONMENT:
Habitats

- Research pictures of habitats – eg, cave, forest, river, garden, underwater
- Draw or trace image on to acetate
- Position overhead projector image on to white wall
- Use in conjunction with textures and sounds

Theme

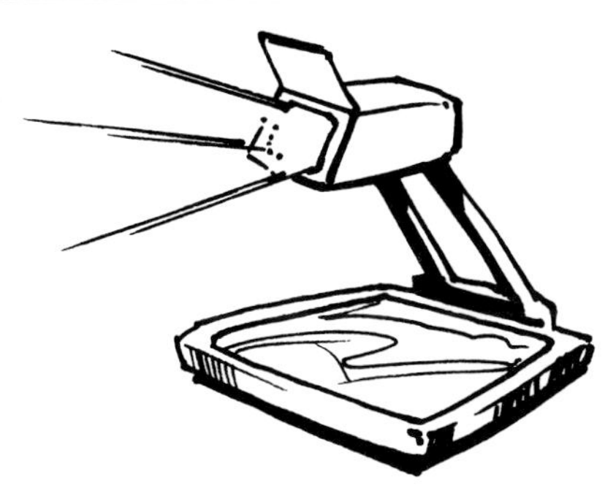

Take an overhead projector

ART & TEXTILES:
Silhouettes

- Create static images using cardboard shapes
- Draw around hands and cut out
- Select pictures of faces in profile from magazines and cut out
- Photograph individuals in profile, enlarge on photocopier and cut out

COMMUNICATION:
Literacy Skills

- Draw around hands on the same piece of acetate
- Write initial on to acetate
- Write name on to acetate
- Play Letter Snap on overhead projector using cardboard letters
- Select pieces of writing to read – adverts, story, poem, articles, original composition

WORKSHEET 1

THEME: TAKE AN OVERHEAD PROJECTOR
Drama – Shadow Screen

FOCUS OBJECTIVES

- To encourage self-expression through body movement
- To develop spatial awareness
- To develop an understanding of cause and effect
- To locate and focus on a moving image
- To participate in group work

EQUIPMENT

Overhead projector
Extension lead and power-breaker
Large white sheet
Card, ribbon, crêpe paper, tissue paper, etc
Scissors
Sticky tape
Cassette player and music

METHOD

1. Choose a theme – for example, Chinese New Year, Christmas Dragon Dance.
2. Cut out the shape of a dragon's head from a large piece of card.
3. Cut lengths of ribbon, or crêpe paper, and attach to a tube of card to make ribbon-sticks.
4. Suspend a white sheet in front of a table with the overhead projector on.
5. Leave enough space between the sheet and the overhead projector to create a large shadow.
6. Explore movement on the screen by walking between the overhead projector and the screen.
7. Place a ribbon on the surface of the overhead projector and pull it across slowly.
8. Stand behind the screen and move a ribbon stick in circular motions and to music.
9. Create a dragon dance and perform behind the screen to music.
10. Use live or recorded music.

This page may be photocopied for instructional use only. *Themed Activities for People with Learning Difficulties* © M Hutchinson 2003

RECORDING SHEET 1

THEME: TAKE AN OVERHEAD PROJECTOR
Drama – Shadow Screen

Name: ______________________ Date: ______________________

FOCUS OBJECTIVES	OBSERVATIONS AND COMMENTS
To encourage self-expression through body movement	
To develop spatial awareness	
To develop an understanding of cause and effect	
To locate and focus on a moving image	
To participate in group work	

This page may be photocopied for instructional use only. *Themed Activities for People with Learning Difficulties* © M Hutchinson 2003

WORKSHEET 2

THEME: TAKE AN OVERHEAD PROJECTOR
The Environment – Habitats

FOCUS OBJECTIVES

- To develop an awareness of surroundings
- To develop visual tracking
- To develop listening skills
- To encourage tactile exploration
- To encourage passing skills

EQUIPMENT

Overhead projector
Extension lead and power-breaker
Overhead projector acetate sheets and pens
Large pieces of plain paper
Resource books/magazines – pond, forest, garden, desert, etc
Collage materials – cardboard, material, bubble-wrap, etc
Pencil
Scissors
PVA glue/glue stick
Large piece of card

METHOD

1. Secure a large sheet of paper on a wall.
2. Position the overhead projector on a table in front of the sheet of paper.
3. Select a habitat to explore from the resource materials.
4. Draw a rough outline of the habitat on to a sheet of acetate.
5. Place the acetate on to the overhead projector, and position the image on the sheet of paper on the wall.
6. Move the overhead projector nearer or further away from the paper on the wall until the image covers most of the paper.
7. Draw around the image on the paper.
8. Use the outline as a guide to create a collage of the habitat.
9. Glue the finished collage on to a sheet of card to be displayed.

Speechmark  This page may be photocopied for instructional use only. *Themed Activities for People with Learning Difficulties* © M Hutchinson 2003

RECORDING SHEET 2

THEME: TAKE AN OVERHEAD PROJECTOR
The Environment – Habitats

Name: ______________________ Date: ______________________

FOCUS OBJECTIVES	OBSERVATIONS AND COMMENTS
To develop an awareness of surroundings	
To develop visual tracking	
To develop listening skills	
To encourage tactile exploration	
To encourage passing skills	

This page may be photocopied for instructional use only. *Themed Activities for People with Learning Difficulties* © M Hutchinson 2003

WORKSHEET 3

THEME: TAKE AN OVERHEAD PROJECTOR
Art & Textiles – Silhouettes

FOCUS OBJECTIVES

- To develop grasp and release
- To develop eye contact
- To develop concentration span
- To encourage participation in group projects
- To develop turn-taking skills

EQUIPMENT

Thin card or paper
Felt pens
Scissors
Magazines
Overhead projector
Extension lead and power-breaker
Doily

METHOD

1. Draw around hands on the thin card or paper.
2. Cut out shapes and write the owner's name on each one.
3. Set up the overhead projector on a table in front of a clear piece of wall.
4. Place each hand-shape, in turn, on the overhead projector. Encourage individuals to guess whose hand silhouette it is.
5. Photograph individuals in profile and enlarge images on a photocopier.
6. Place each profile on the overhead projector in turn.
7. Talk about how each one is different.
8. Look through magazines for pictures of faces in profile, and everyday objects: car, cup, chair, saucepan, etc.
9. Cut out chosen pictures.
10. Place one at a time on the overhead projector.
11. Identify each object from its silhouette.

Speechmark P This page may be photocopied for instructional use only. *Themed Activities for People with Learning Difficulties* © M Hutchinson 2003

RECORDING SHEET 3

THEME: TAKE AN OVERHEAD PROJECTOR
Art & Textiles – Silhouettes

Name: ______________________ Date: ______________

FOCUS OBJECTIVES	OBSERVATIONS AND COMMENTS
To develop grasp and release	
To develop eye contact	
To develop concentration span	
To encourage participation in group projects	
To develop turn-taking skills	

This page may be photocopied for instructional use only. *Themed Activities for People with Learning Difficulties* © M Hutchinson 2003

WORKSHEET 4 | THEME: TAKE AN OVERHEAD PROJECTOR

Communication – Literacy Skills

FOCUS OBJECTIVES

- To develop acceptance of touch
- To develop matching skills
- To develop an awareness of self and others
- To recognise own initials or name when written down
- To have opportunities to make choices

EQUIPMENT

Overhead projector
Extension lead and power-breaker
Overhead projector acetate sheets
Selection of coloured pens
Resource books – short stories, poems, etc
Large piece of paper
Card
Craft knife and cutting board
Sheets of plain paper

METHOD

1 Draw around one hand of each person in the group on the same piece of acetate. The outlines can overlap if each one is in a different colour.
2 Place the acetate on the overhead projector and position the image on a large piece of paper on the wall.
3 Draw around each hand outline, in the same colour, on the piece of paper.
4 Encourage individuals to identify their hand and 'sign' their name next to it on the sheet of paper.
5 Cut out the letters of the alphabet in card and place next to the overhead projector.
6 Write each letter of the alphabet on a sheet of paper.
7 Select a cardboard letter and place on the overhead projector.
8 Ask the group to look through the paper letters until they find the matching letter.
9 Continue with other letters of the alphabet.

Speechmark P This page may be photocopied for instructional use only. *Themed Activities for People with Learning Difficulties* © M Hutchinson 2003

RECORDING SHEET 4

THEME: TAKE AN OVERHEAD PROJECTOR
Communication – Literacy Skills

Name: Date:

FOCUS OBJECTIVES	OBSERVATIONS AND COMMENTS
To develop acceptance of touch	
To develop matching skills	
To develop an awareness of self and others	
To recognise own initials or name when written down	
To have opportunities to make choices	

This page may be photocopied for instructional use only. *Themed Activities for People with Learning Difficulties* © M Hutchinson 2003

THE ENVIRONMENT:
Conservation

- Research a design for a bird-box
- Measure and cut wood
- Sand wood
- Construct bird-box
- Paint and varnish bird-box
- Position and secure bird-box in garden

MUSIC:
Rhythm Sticks

- Cut lengths of dowelling to make music sticks
- Sand ends of dowelling
- Decorate sticks with paint
- Varnish sticks
- Use sticks to explore rhythm

Theme

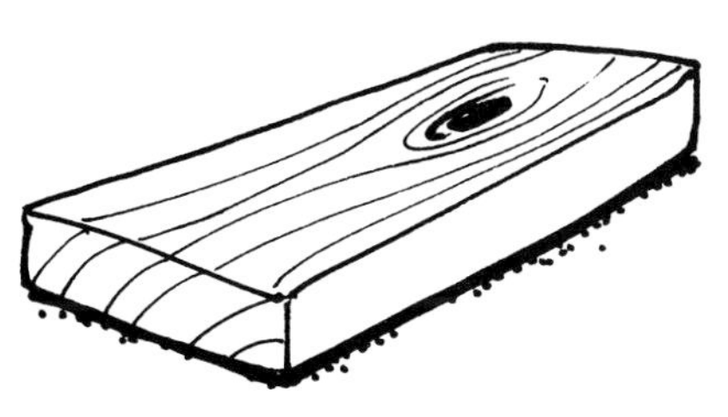

Take a piece of wood

ART & TEXTILES:
Picture-Framing

- Select wood
- Measure and cut wood
- Fix pieces of wood together
- Mount picture on to mounting board
- Secure picture in the frame

COMMUNITY LIVING:
Shopping Skills

- Measure the picture to be framed
- Make a shopping list
- Match items on the list to real objects
- Use a shopping trolley
- Queue and pay for items
- Transfer items from trolley to car

WORKSHEET 1

THEME: TAKE A PIECE OF WOOD
The Environment – Conservation

FOCUS OBJECTIVES

- To develop hand-eye coordination
- To explore shapes and textures
- To develop sequencing skills
- To use woodwork equipment
- To develop decision-making skills

EQUIPMENT

Resource books – carpentry, making bird-boxes, about birds
Ruler and pencil
Plywood
PVA glue
Hammer and panel pins
Sandpaper
Paint and varnish
Paintbrushes
Newspaper for covering tables
Apron
Saw

METHOD

1. Select a bird-box from the resource books.
2. Follow the template provided or design your own.
3. Cover the table you are working on with newspaper.
4. Draw the design on to 6 mm (¼ in) thick plywood.
5. Cut out the pieces and sand the edges.
6. Assemble the pieces using the PVA glue and panel pins.
7. Paint the bird-box.
8. When dry, varnish.
9. Place the bird-box in a quiet and shady place in the garden at a height of approximately 2 m (6 ft).

This page may be photocopied for instructional use only. *Themed Activities for People with Learning Difficulties* © M Hutchinson 2003

Speechmark

RECORDING SHEET 1

THEME: TAKE A PIECE OF WOOD
The Environment – Conservation

Name: ______________________ Date: ______________________

FOCUS OBJECTIVES	OBSERVATIONS AND COMMENTS
To develop hand-eye coordination	
To explore shapes and textures	
To develop sequencing skills	
To use woodwork equipment	
To develop decision-making skills	

This page may be photocopied for instructional use only. *Themed Activities for People with Learning Difficulties* © M Hutchinson 2003

Speechmark

WORKSHEET 2

THEME: TAKE A PIECE OF WOOD
Music – Making Rhythm Sticks

FOCUS OBJECTIVES

- To develop sequencing skills
- To develop hand-eye coordination
- To encourage choice and decision-making
- To develop listening skills
- To develop peer group interaction

EQUIPMENT

Length of thick dowelling – approximately 153 cm (60 in)
Ruler and pencil
Saw
Sandpaper
Masking tape
Paint and varnish
Paintbrushes
Newspaper
Tape recorder and blank tape

METHOD

1. Secure the dowelling to the table with the masking tape.
2. Measure 25 cm (10 in) along the dowelling and mark with a pencil – start from the left-hand end of the dowelling.
3. Repeat this process five more times.
4. Remove the dowelling from the table and cut into the six measured lengths.
5. Sand the ends of each piece.
6. Divide into three pairs.
7. Paint each pair a different colour or pattern.
8. Varnish when dry.
9. Use the sticks to create different rhythms and sound patterns. Try tapping out the syllables in peoples' names.
10. Encourage individuals to start a rhythm for others to repeat.
11. Record the rhythms and play back to the group.

Speechmark  This page may be photocopied for instructional use only. *Themed Activities for People with Learning Difficulties* © M Hutchinson 2003

RECORDING SHEET 2

THEME: TAKE A PIECE OF WOOD
Music – Making Rhythm Sticks

Name: ______________________ Date: ______________________

FOCUS OBJECTIVES	OBSERVATIONS AND COMMENTS
To develop sequencing skills	
To develop hand-eye coordination	
To encourage choice and decision-making	
To develop listening skills	
To develop peer group interaction	

This page may be photocopied for instructional use only. *Themed Activities for People with Learning Difficulties* © M Hutchinson 2003

WORKSHEET 3 | THEME: TAKE A PIECE OF WOOD

Art & textiles – Picture-Framing

FOCUS OBJECTIVES

- To develop choice-making skills
- To develop measuring skills
- To develop sequencing skills
- To increase concentration span
- To develop an understanding of cause and effect

EQUIPMENT

Resource books – picture-framing, wood and carpentry, etc
Length of wood
Ruler and pencil
Saw
Sandpaper
Thick card
PVA glue/glue stick
4 flat brackets, hammer and panel pins

METHOD

1 Choose a picture or piece of work to be framed. As no glass is involved, the picture does not need to be flat.
2 Decide on the proportions of the frame and write down the measurements.
3 Select and buy the wood.
4 Measure and cut four pieces from the length of wood and sand any rough surfaces.
5 Use the brackets, hammer and panel pins to secure each corner of the frame.
6 Trim the thick card so that it is 0.5 cm (1 in) larger than the inside measurement of the frame.
7 Glue the picture to the trimmed card.
8 Turn the frame upside down and position the card and picture face down on to the frame.
9 Secure the card to the frame using the masking tape.

Speechmark  This page may be photocopied for instructional use only. *Themed Activities for People with Learning Difficulties* © M Hutchinson 2003

RECORDING SHEET 3

THEME: TAKE A PIECE OF WOOD
Art & textiles – Picture-Framing

Name: Date:

FOCUS OBJECTIVES	OBSERVATIONS AND COMMENTS
To develop choice-making skills	
To develop measuring skills	
To develop sequencing skills	
To increase concentration span	
To develop an understanding of cause and effect	

This page may be photocopied for instructional use only. *Themed Activities for People with Learning Difficulties* © M Hutchinson 2003

WORKSHEET 4

THEME: TAKE A PIECE OF WOOD
Community Living – Shopping Skills

FOCUS OBJECTIVES

- To have opportunities to make choices
- To develop matching skills
- To develop confidence in a variety of community-based settings
- To develop waiting skills
- To work on literacy and numeracy skills

EQUIPMENT

Pen and paper
Purse/wallet with money
Shopping bag
Transport
Photographs/pictures of wood, nails, sandpaper, etc
DIY catalogues

METHOD

Preparation for Trip

1 Write a list using written, pictorial and symbolic forms.
2 Measure the length of wood needed.
3 Count out money and place in a purse or wallet.
4 Look at DIY catalogues and pictures.
5 Find out where the nearest DIY shop is.
6 Talk about the journey to the shop.

Buying the Wood

1 Find a trolley and look at the shopping list.
2 Walk around the shop and locate the wood section.
3 Select the correct size piece of wood.
4 Find the other items on the shopping list.
5 Pay for the items at a checkout.
6 Wait for the receipt and any change.

This page may be photocopied for instructional use only. *Themed Activities for People with Learning Difficulties* © M Hutchinson 2003

RECORDING SHEET 4

THEME: TAKE A PIECE OF WOOD
Community Living – Shopping Skills

Name:

Date:

FOCUS OBJECTIVES	OBSERVATIONS AND COMMENTS
To have opportunities to make choices	
To develop matching skills	
To develop confidence in a variety of community-based settings	
To work on literacy and numeracy skills	

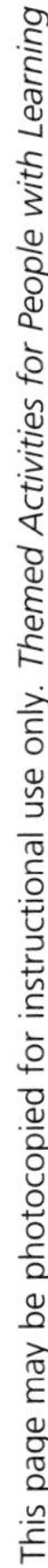
This page may be photocopied for instructional use only. *Themed Activities for People with Learning Difficulties* © M Hutchinson 2003

COOKING:
Fresh Orange Juice

- Buy large oranges
- Wash the oranges
- Cut oranges into halves
- Use a juicer to squeeze oranges
- Pour juice into a jug
- Sieve if necessary
- Chill in the fridge
- Drink

THE ENVIRONMENT
Recycling

- Collect all orange peel, pith, pips, etc from squeezing oranges
- Put into a plastic bag or bucket
- Take to an existing compost bin or start one
- Add orange peel to the compost bin

Theme

Take an orange

ART & TEXTILES:
Pomanders

- Select small oranges
- Wash and dry oranges
- Tie narrow ribbon around the oranges
- Attach a loop of ribbon at the top of each orange
- Make holes in oranges with a fork
- Push cloves into the holes

COMMUNICATION:
Numeracy Skills

- Identify coins required for purchase
- Put money into purse or wallet
- Go to supermarket
- Find and price the oranges
- Take the oranges to the checkout
- Select correct money and pay for oranges

WORKSHEET 1

THEME: TAKE AN ORANGE
Cooking – Fresh Orange Juice

FOCUS OBJECTIVES

- To develop grasp and release
- To encourage passing skills
- To develop sequencing skills
- To extend experiences of taste and smell
- To develop an awareness of safety and hygiene

EQUIPMENT

6–8 large oranges
Bowl of cold water
Clean tea-towel
Juicer – manual or electric with power-breaker
Jug
Knife and chopping board
Apron

METHOD

1. Wash and dry the oranges.
2. Cut each orange in half using the knife and chopping board.
3. Place the cut oranges into a large bowl.
4. Squeeze all the oranges using either a manual or electric juicer.
5. Pour the juice into a jug and place in the fridge.
6. Serve chilled.

Safety and Hygiene

1. Wash hands before activity.
2. Wear apron to protect clothing.
3. Talk about how to use sharp knives.
4. Keep surfaces and utensils clean.
5. Use a power-breaker with any electrical equipment.

Speechmark  This page may be photocopied for instructional use only. *Themed Activities for People with Learning Difficulties* © M Hutchinson 2003

RECORDING SHEET 1

THEME: TAKE AN ORANGE
Cooking – Fresh Orange Juice

Name: ______________________ Date: ______________________

FOCUS OBJECTIVES	OBSERVATIONS AND COMMENTS
To develop grasp and release	
To encourage passing skills	
To develop sequencing skills	
To extend experiences of taste and smell	
To develop an awareness of safety and hygiene	

This page may be photocopied for instructional use only. *Themed Activities for People with Learning Difficulties* © M Hutchinson 2003
Speechmark

WORKSHEET 2 | THEME: TAKE AN ORANGE

The Environment – Recycling

FOCUS OBJECTIVES

- To develop object recognition
- To develop hand-eye coordination
- To develop sequencing skills
- To encourage exploration through the senses
- To develop matching skills

EQUIPMENT

Information about making and using a compost bin
Large sheet of paper
Felt pens
Food magazines
Scissors
Glue stick
Bucket or plastic bag
Orange skins, pith and pips

METHOD

1. If you already have a compost bin, collect all the orange skins, pith and pips from squeezing the oranges, and place them in a bucket or plastic bag.
2. Take the bucket or plastic bag to the compost bin and tip in contents.
3. If you need to start a compost bin, find out what is required.
4. Make a list of equipment that is needed and obtain it.
5. Make a list of what can be put into a compost bin.
6. Look through food magazines for pictures of fruit and vegetables and cut them out.
7. Draw an outline of a compost bin on a large sheet of paper.
8. Glue the pictures of fruit and vegetables inside the outline of the compost bin to create a poster.

Speechmark P This page may be photocopied for instructional use only. *Themed Activities for People with Learning Difficulties* © M Hutchinson 2003

RECORDING SHEET 2

THEME: TAKE AN ORANGE
The Environment – Recycling

Name: ______________________ Date: ______________________

FOCUS OBJECTIVES	OBSERVATIONS AND COMMENTS
To develop object recognition	
To develop hand-eye coordination	
To develop sequencing skills	
To encourage exploration through the senses	
To develop matching skills	

This page may be photocopied for instructional use only. *Themed Activities for People with Learning Difficulties* © M Hutchinson 2003

WORKSHEET 3

THEME: TAKE AN ORANGE
Art & Textiles – Pomanders

FOCUS OBJECTIVES

- To develop matching skills
- To develop pincer grip
- To develop sequencing skills
- To provide opportunities to explore a range of smells
- To develop fine motor skills

EQUIPMENT

3–4 small oranges
Bowl of cold water
Tea-towel
Fork
Small box of cloves
Ribbon
Scissors
Small bowl

METHOD

1 Wash and dry the oranges.
2 Tip the cloves into a small bowl.
3 Take an orange and tie a piece of ribbon around the middle of it. Knot it securely.
4 Trim the ends.
5 Tie a longer piece of ribbon around the orange, crossing the first ribbon, leaving four areas of uncovered skin.
6 Use the extra ribbon to make a loop to hang the orange from.
7 Prick each quarter of the skin with the fork, about eight times, to make holes.
8 Take a clove and push it into one of the holes.
9 Repeat until all the holes are filled with cloves.

 This page may be photocopied for instructional use only. *Themed Activities for People with Learning Difficulties* © M Hutchinson 2003

RECORDING SHEET 3

THEME: TAKE AN ORANGE
Art & Textiles – Pomanders

Name: ______________________ Date: ______________________

FOCUS OBJECTIVES	OBSERVATIONS AND COMMENTS
To develop matching skills	
To develop pincer grip	
To develop sequencing skills	
To provide opportunities to explore a range of smells	
To develop fine motor skills	

This page may be photocopied for instructional use only. *Themed Activities for People with Learning Difficulties* © M Hutchinson 2003

WORKSHEET 4 | THEME: TAKE AN ORANGE

Communication – Numeracy Skills

FOCUS OBJECTIVES

- To develop observation skills
- To develop matching skills
- To develop confidence in a variety of community-based settings
- To develop waiting skills
- To identify different coin values

EQUIPMENT

Clipboard
Pen and paper
Selection of coins
Purse/wallet
Shopping bag
Transport
Photographs/pictures of oranges

METHOD

1. Make a list of what to buy.
2. Attach the list to the clipboard.
3. Practise coin recognition and value.
4. Count out money and place in purse or wallet.
5. Look at pictures of oranges before going to the shop.
6. In the shop find the fruit section.
7. Match a picture of an orange to a real one.
8. Write the price of one orange on the shopping list attached to the clipboard.
9. Multiply the price of one orange with the number of oranges you are buying.
10. Pay at the checkout.
11. Check your answer against the receipt.

This page may be photocopied for instructional use only. *Themed Activities for People with Learning Difficulties* © M Hutchinson 2003

RECORDING SHEET 4

THEME: TAKE AN ORANGE
Communication – Numeracy Skills

Name: ______________________ Date: ______________________

FOCUS OBJECTIVES	OBSERVATIONS AND COMMENTS
To develop observation skills	
To develop matching skills	
To develop confidence in a variety of community-based settings	
To develop waiting skills	
To identify different coin values	

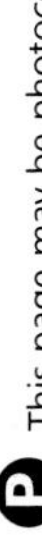

This page may be photocopied for instructional use only. *Themed Activities for People with Learning Difficulties* © M Hutchinson 2003

ART & TEXTILES:
Windchimes

- Buy several thick bamboo sticks
- Measure and cut into six equal lengths
- Make holes at the top of each stick
- Thread cord through
- Attach to central piece of bamboo
- Hang in garden or room

DRAMA:
Ribbon-Sticks

- Use a length of thin bamboo – 40 cm/16 in
- Select a range of coloured ribbons
- Cut into strips of up to 80 cm/32 in long
- Attach to one end of the bamboo stick using brightly coloured insulating tape

Theme

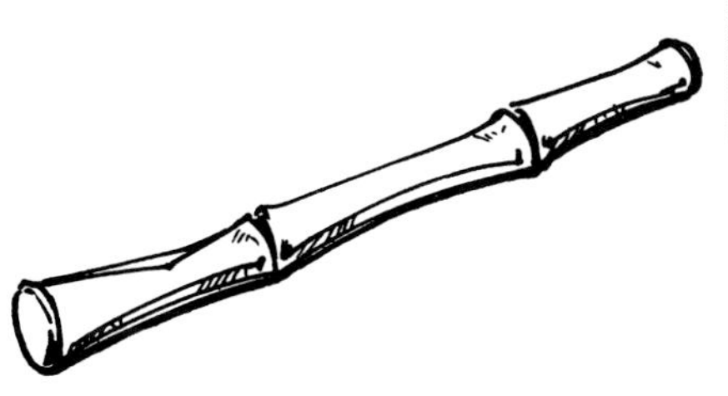

Take a bamboo stick

MUSIC:
Zither

- Use a piece of thick bamboo, cut and sand the ends
- Use a felt pen to mark lines along the bamboo
- With a triangular rasp, file ridges into the bamboo
- Cut a small length of dowelling and use to run up and down ridges

THE ENVIRONMENT:
Plant Frames

- Tie three long lengths of thin bamboo at the top – to make a tripod for sweetpeas
- Cut two bamboo sticks in half
- Tie into a square
- Attach a long bamboo stick to each corner
- Use to grow sunflowers

WORKSHEET 1

THEME: TAKE A BAMBOO STICK
Art & Textiles – Windchimes

FOCUS OBJECTIVES

- To develop listening skills
- To work on numeracy skills
- To develop sequencing skills
- To encourage exploration of art materials and equipment
- To develop threading skills

EQUIPMENT

2–3 thick bamboo sticks
Ruler and pencil
Saw
Sandpaper
Drill
Cord
Scissors

METHOD

1. Measure and cut five equal lengths of bamboo, about 30 cm (12 in) long.
2. Measure and cut two shorter lengths of bamboo, about 20 cm (8 in) long.
3. Sand the ends of each piece.
4. Drill holes at one end only of each longer piece of bamboo.
5. Thread a length of cord through each hole.
6. Secure with a knot – leave the ends above the knot long.
7. Bind the two shorter pieces of bamboo together in a cross shape.
8. Suspend one bamboo stick from the middle of the cross shape, using the excess cord above the knot.
9. Secure to the cross shape with a knot.
10. Repeat with the remaining bamboo sticks, positioning each one at the ends of the cross-shape.
11. Tie a length of cord from the centre of the cross-shape to create a loop to hang the windchime from.

Speechmark P This page may be photocopied for instructional use only. *Themed Activities for People with Learning Difficulties* © M Hutchinson 2003

RECORDING SHEET 1

THEME: TAKE A BAMBOO STICK
Art & Textiles – Windchimes

Name: Date:

FOCUS OBJECTIVES	OBSERVATIONS AND COMMENTS
To develop listening skills	
To work on numeracy skills	
To develop sequencing skills	
To encourage exploration of art materials and equipment	
To develop threading skills	

This page may be photocopied for instructional use only. *Themed Activities for People with Learning Difficulties* © M Hutchinson 2003

WORKSHEET 2

THEME: TAKE A BAMBOO STICK
Drama – Ribbon-Sticks

FOCUS OBJECTIVES

- To encourage extending and rotating the arm
- To develop visual tracking
- To encourage choice-making
- To develop self-awareness
- To encourage participation in group work

EQUIPMENT

Thin bamboo sticks
Selection of coloured ribbons
Scissors
Ruler
Coloured insulating tape
Sandpaper
Saw
Shredder and power-breaker
Tissue paper – various colours
Cassette player and tapes

METHOD

1. Cut the bamboo sticks into lengths of 40 cm (16 in).
2. Sand the ends of each stick.
3. Choose 2–3 different colours of ribbon.
4. Cut into strips of up to 80 cm (32 in).
5. Attach about 8–10 strips to one end of a bamboo stick, using the insulating tape.
6. Alternatively – fold sheets of tissue paper and feed through a shredder.
7. Attach a selection of coloured lengths of tissue to a bamboo stick with the tape.
8. The tissue-paper sticks will make a different sound from the ribbon-sticks.
9. Move the ribbon and tissue-paper sticks to gentle music.

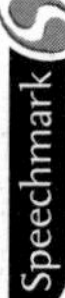

Speechmark This page may be photocopied for instructional use only. *Themed Activities for People with Learning Difficulties* © M Hutchinson 2003

RECORDING SHEET 2

THEME: TAKE A BAMBOO STICK
Drama – Ribbon-Sticks

Name: ______________________ Date: ______________________

FOCUS OBJECTIVES	OBSERVATIONS AND COMMENTS
To encourage extending and rotating the arm	
To develop visual tracking	
To encourage choice-making	
To develop self-awareness	
To encourage participation in group work	

This page may be photocopied for instructional use only. *Themed Activities for People with Learning Difficulties* © M Hutchinson 2003

WORKSHEET 3

THEME: TAKE A BAMBOO STICK
Music – Zither

FOCUS OBJECTIVES

- To have opportunities to use woodwork equipment
- To develop listening skills
- To develop sequencing skills
- To encourage self-expression
- To develop fine motor skills

EQUIPMENT

Length of thick bamboo
Saw
Sandpaper
Ruler and felt pen
Triangular rasp
Dowelling
Cassette recorder and blank tape

METHOD

1. Cut the bamboo to a length of 30 cm (12 in).
2. Sand the ends of the bamboo.
3. Measure 4 cm (1½ in) in from each end of the bamboo and mark with a felt pen.
4. Measure and mark every 2 cm (¾ in) along the bamboo, between the lines you have drawn.
5. Make a shallow cut on each line marked, using the saw.
6. Widen each cut into a ridge with the triangular rasp.
7. Cut a short piece of dowelling and sand the ends.
8. Use the dowelling to run up and down the ridges on the bamboo to create a pattern of sound.
9. Make more bamboo zithers in a range of sizes, and explore how they sound different.
10. Compose a piece of music as a group.
11. Record and play back to the group.

Speechmark  This page may be photocopied for instructional use only. *Themed Activities for People with Learning Difficulties* © M Hutchinson 2003

RECORDING SHEET 3

THEME: TAKE A BAMBOO STICK
Music – Zither

Name: ______________________ Date: ______________________

FOCUS OBJECTIVES	OBSERVATIONS AND COMMENTS
To have opportunities to use woodwork equipment	
To develop listening skills	
To develop sequencing skills	
To encourage self-expression	
To develop fine motor skills	

This page may be photocopied for instructional use only. *Themed Activities for People with Learning Difficulties* © M Hutchinson 2003

WORKSHEET 4

THEME: TAKE A BAMBOO STICK
The Environment – Plant Frames

FOCUS OBJECTIVES

- To have opportunities to explore different textures
- To develop hand-eye coordination
- To develop recognition skills
- To develop listening skills
- To develop measuring skills

EQUIPMENT

9 long bamboo sticks
Garden twine
Scissors
Flowerpots
Sweetpea plants
4 sunflower seedlings

METHOD

Tripod for Sweetpeas

1 Hold together three long bamboo sticks.
2 Tie together with the twine – about a quarter of the way down the sticks. Allow for some movement of the sticks.
3 Gently pull out the bottom ends of the sticks to make a free-standing tripod shape.
4 Secure the sticks in this position by binding them at the top very tightly with more twine.
5 Place over flowerpots or flowerbeds with sweetpea plants in.

Sunflower Frame

1 Cut two long bamboo sticks in half.
2 Tie the four pieces into a square with the twine.
3 Attach a long bamboo stick to each corner of the square.
4 Position the frame in the garden with a sunflower plant at the base of each leg.

This page may be photocopied for instructional use only. *Themed Activities for People with Learning Difficulties* © M Hutchinson 2003

RECORDING SHEET 4

THEME: TAKE A BAMBOO STICK
The Environment – Plant Frames

Name: ______________________ Date: ______________________

FOCUS OBJECTIVES	OBSERVATIONS AND COMMENTS
To have opportunities to explore different textures	
To develop hand-eye coordination	
To develop recognition skills	
To develop listening skills	
To develop measuring skills	

This page may be photocopied for instructional use only. *Themed Activities for People with Learning Difficulties* © M Hutchinson 2003

ART & TEXTILES:
Marbling

- Pour water into shallow tray
- Select 2–3 colours from oil-based paint
- With a fork or stick create patterns with the paint floating on the water
- Lay paper on to paint
- Lift off paper to reveal transferred pattern

THE ENVIRONMENT:
Watering Plants

- Take watering can to tap
- Hold under tap
- Turn on tap
- When watering-can is full turn off tap
- Carry watering-can to plants
- Position spout and tip watering can to allow water to come out

Theme

Take a jug of water

COOKING:
Pasta and Vegetables

- Pour water into a saucepan
- Bring to boil and add pasta
- Prepare vegetables and place in steamer
- Position steamer on top of saucepan
- When cooked, strain pasta and serve with vegetables

SCIENCE & TECHNOLOGY:
Properties of Water

- Fill an ice-cube tray or bag and put in freezer
- When frozen, compare ice cubes with water
- Watch ice cubes melting
- Boil a kettle of water
- Watch steam coming out of spout
- Make a hot drink

WORKSHEET 1

THEME: TAKE A JUG OF WATER
Art & Textiles – Marbling

FOCUS OBJECTIVES

- To provide opportunities to make choices
- To develop spatial awareness
- To develop sequencing skills
- To encourage exploration of art materials and equipment
- To develop colour recognition and matching

EQUIPMENT

Jug of water
Shallow tray – 5 cms (2 in) deep and larger than a sheet of paper
Yoghurt pots
Old paintbrush and/or fork
Newspaper
Masking tape
Sheets of white of paper
Aprons – one for each group member
White spirit

METHOD

1. Cover the tables with newspaper.
2. Fill the shallow tray with water – about three-quarters full.
3. Place the tray in the middle of the table.
4. Mix the paint with small amounts of white spirit until fairly runny. Use a separate yoghurt pot for each colour.
5. Choose 2 or 3 colours, and pour a little of each on to the surface of the water.
6. Move the colours around the surface of the water, using the handle of an old paintbrush or a fork to create a pattern.
7. Gently place a piece of paper on to the surface of the water.
8. Peel the paper off the water very slowly – start with one corner, and place on a sheet of newspaper, pattern side up, to dry.
9. Add more paint for each print.

Health and Safety

1. Keep the white spirit out of reach of group members at all times.
2. Wear aprons to protect clothing from oil-based paint.
3. Carefully dispose of all yoghurt pots when this activity is finished – tie securely in a plastic bag that will not leak in the rubbish.

This page may be photocopied for instructional use only. *Themed Activities for People with Learning Difficulties* © M Hutchinson 2003

RECORDING SHEET 1

THEME: TAKE A JUG OF WATER
Art & Textiles – Marbling

Name: Date:

FOCUS OBJECTIVES	OBSERVATIONS AND COMMENTS
To provide opportunities to make choices	
To develop spatial awareness	
To develop sequencing skills	
To encourage exploration of art materials and equipment	
To develop colour recognition and matching	

Speechmark This page may be photocopied for instructional use only. *Themed Activities for People with Learning Difficulties* © M Hutchinson 2003

WORKSHEET 2

THEME: TAKE A JUG OF WATER
The Environment – Watering Plants

FOCUS OBJECTIVES

- To develop grasp and release
- To develop hand-eye coordination
- To encourage tactile exploration
- To develop sequencing skills
- To encourage participation in a task

EQUIPMENT

Access to a tap
Watering-can
Plants to water
Apron

METHOD

1. Put on apron to protect clothing.
2. Take the watering-can to the tap.
3. Hold the watering-can under the tap, stand it in the sink, or put it on the ground (if using an outside tap).
4. Turn on the cold tap.
5. Fill the watering-can as full as is needed or can be carried.
6. Turn off the tap.
7. Hold the watering-can by the handle and support at the base, as required.
8. Carry the watering-can to the plants.
9. Position the spout of the watering-can at the base of the plants.
10. Tilt the watering-can from the handle to allow the water to come out.
11. Repeat the process when the watering-can is empty.

Speechmark This page may be photocopied for instructional use only. *Themed Activities for People with Learning Difficulties* © M Hutchinson 2003

RECORDING SHEET 2

THEME: TAKE A JUG OF WATER
The Environment – Watering Plants

Name: ______________________ Date: ______________________

FOCUS OBJECTIVES	OBSERVATIONS AND COMMENTS
To develop grasp and release	
To develop hand-eye coordination	
To encourage tactile exploration	
To develop sequencing skills	
To encourage participation in a task	

This page may be photocopied for instructional use only. *Themed Activities for People with Learning Difficulties* © M Hutchinson 2003

WORKSHEET 3

THEME: TAKE A JUG OF WATER
Cooking – Pasta and Vegetables

FOCUS OBJECTIVES

- To extend experiences of taste and smell
- To develop an awareness of safety and hygiene
- To develop sequencing skills
- To explore textures of raw and cooked food
- To develop fine motor skills

EQUIPMENT

Large saucepan
Serving bowl
Wooden spoon
Tablespoon
Olive oil
Knife and chopping board
Tomato purée (optional)
Vegetables – broccoli, courgette, carrot, cauliflower
Salt
Two-tier vegetable steamer
Aprons – one for each group member

METHOD

1. Fill the saucepan with water and bring to the boil.
2. Add the pasta to the water with a tablespoon of olive oil and salt to taste.
3. Wash the vegetables and cut into small pieces.
4. Place the vegetables into the two tiers of the steamer.
5. Carefully position the steamer on top of the saucepan.
6. When the pasta is cooked, remove and strain. The vegetables should also be cooked.
7. Tip the pasta into a serving bowl.
8. Add a tablespoon of tomato purée and the vegetables. Mix well and serve.

Safety and Hygiene

1. Wash hands before activity.
2. Talk about how to use sharp knives.
3. Discuss the position of the saucepan on the cooker.

Speechmark P This page may be photocopied for instructional use only. *Themed Activities for People with Learning Difficulties* © M Hutchinson 2003

RECORDING SHEET 3

THEME: TAKE A JUG OF WATER
Cooking – Pasta and Vegetables

Name: ______________________ Date: ______________________

FOCUS OBJECTIVES	OBSERVATIONS AND COMMENTS
To extend experiences of taste and smell	
To develop an awareness of safety and hygiene	
To develop sequencing skills	
To explore textures of raw and cooked food	
To develop fine motor skills	

Speechmark This page may be photocopied for instructional use only. *Themed Activities for People with Learning Difficulties* © M Hutchinson 2003

WORKSHEET 4

THEME: TAKE A JUG OF WATER
Science & Technology – Properties of Water

FOCUS OBJECTIVES

- To develop observation skills
- To encourage exploration through the senses
- To develop fine motor skills
- To develop waiting skills
- To encourage eye contact

EQUIPMENT

Ice-cube tray or bag
Food colouring – red, blue, green, etc
Large glass bowl
Kettle
Cup
Spoon
Tea/coffee, etc

METHOD

Ice Cubes

1 Fill an ice-cube tray or bag with a selection of coloured water (mix food colouring in with the water), and freeze.
2 Feel the ice cubes and compare with water to see which is colder.
3 Fill a large glass bowl with water.
4 Drop the coloured ice-cubes into the water.
5 Watch the ice-cubes melting.

Making a Drink

1 Fill the kettle with water and switch on.
2 While the kettle is boiling, prepare a drink.
3 Watch the steam as the hot water is poured into the cup.

Safety and Hygiene

1 Wash hands before activity.
2 Talk about using boiling water.

Speechmark This page may be photocopied for instructional use only. *Themed Activities for People with Learning Difficulties* © M Hutchinson 2003

RECORDING SHEET 4

THEME: TAKE A JUG OF WATER
Science & Technology – Properties of Water

Name:

Date:

FOCUS OBJECTIVES	OBSERVATIONS AND COMMENTS
To develop observation skills	
To encourage exploration through the senses	
To develop fine motor skills	
To develop waiting skills	
To encourage eye contact	

This page may be photocopied for instructional use only. *Themed Activities for People with Learning Difficulties* © M Hutchinson 2003

COOKING:
Spicy Potatoes

- Research recipe and ingredients
- Wash and peel potatoes
- Smell and taste spices
- Cook potatoes
- Add remaining ingredients
- Choose a serving dish
- Place cooked spicy potatoes in dish and serve

THE ENVIRONMENT:
Gardening

- Prepare a large tub for planting
- Fill tub with compost – $^3/_4$ full
- Place seed potatoes in tub
- Cover with a thick layer of compost
- Water
- Place out of doors

Theme

Take a potato

SCIENCE & TECHNOLOGY:
Investigating Potatoes

- Look at 3 or 4 different kinds of potato – King Edward, sweet potato, Anya, new potatoes
- Draw each kind of potato
- Describe the size, shape, colour and texture of each
- Take photographs of each potato and make a poster

COMMUNITY LIVING:
Shopping

- Write list of different kinds of potatoes to buy
- Talk about which shops will sell potatoes – supermarket, greengrocer, garden centre, DIY store
- Find pictures of different kinds of potatoes in magazines, and make a pictorial shopping list
- Buy the potatoes

WORKSHEET 1

THEME: TAKE A POTATO
Cooking – Spicy Potatoes

FOCUS OBJECTIVES

- To extend experiences of taste and smell
- To develop hand-eye coordination
- To develop sequencing skills
- To develop waiting skills
- To develop an awareness of safety and hygiene

EQUIPMENT

Potatoes
Peeler
Recipe
Ingredients – chilli powder, cardamom pods, pepper, small onion, green and red sweet peppers
Cooking oil
Large frying pan or wok and spatula
Saucepan
Knife and chopping board
Aprons – one for each group member

METHOD

1 Wash and peel potatoes.
2 Cut into small pieces and boil in a saucepan of water.
3 Finely chop the small onion and the sweet peppers.
4 Heat a small amount of cooking oil in the frying pan/wok.
5 Add 2 or 3 cardamom pods, chopped onion and peppers.
6 Fry until the onions are soft.
7 When the potatoes are cooked, drain and add to the frying pan/wok.
8 Mix together the potatoes and vegetables. Add chilli powder to taste.

Safety and Hygiene

1 Wash hands before activity.
2 Talk about how to work with hot water and fat.
3 Wear aprons to protect clothing.
4 Be sure not to touch your eyes when cutting the onion and sweet peppers.
5 Wash hands after activity.

Speechmark  This page may be photocopied for instructional use only. *Themed Activities for People with Learning Difficulties* © M Hutchinson 2003

RECORDING SHEET 1

THEME: TAKE A POTATO
Cooking – Spicy Potatoes

Name: ____________________ Date: ____________________

FOCUS OBJECTIVES	OBSERVATIONS AND COMMENTS
To extend experiences of taste and smell	
To develop hand-eye coordination	
To develop sequencing skills	
To develop waiting skills	
To develop an awareness of safety and hygiene	

Speechmark P This page may be photocopied for instructional use only. *Themed Activities for People with Learning Difficulties* © M Hutchinson 2003

WORKSHEET 2

THEME: TAKE A POTATO
The Environment – Gardening

FOCUS OBJECTIVES

- To develop observation skills
- To encourage tactile exploration
- To develop environmental awareness
- To develop sequencing skills
- To encourage participation in group activities

EQUIPMENT

Large planting tub
Compost
Trowel
Seed potatoes
Watering-can
Label for the tub
Waterproof pen
Apron
Broken clay flowerpots

METHOD

1. Prepare a large tub for planting – position it in a sunny place in the garden.
2. Put some broken flowerpots in the bottom of the tub for drainage.
3. Fill the tub with compost – about three-quarters full.
4. Position the seed potatoes in the compost – leave spaces between them.
5. Cover the seed potatoes with a thick layer of compost.
6. Water the tub.
7. Make a label for the tub – note the type of potatoes growing and the date they were planted.
8. Water the plants as they grow.
9. A few weeks after the plants have flowered, feel into the compost to see if any new potatoes are growing.
10. Harvest the potatoes, cook and eat them.

Speechmark  This page may be photocopied for instructional use only. *Themed Activities for People with Learning Difficulties* © M Hutchinson 2003

RECORDING SHEET 2

THEME: TAKE A POTATO
The Environment – Gardening

Name: Date:

FOCUS OBJECTIVES	OBSERVATIONS AND COMMENTS
To develop observation skills	
To encourage tactile exploration	
To develop environmental awareness	
To develop sequencing skills	
To encourage participation in group activities	

This page may be photocopied for instructional use only. *Themed Activities for People with Learning Difficulties* © M Hutchinson 2003

WORKSHEET 3

THEME: TAKE A POTATO
Science & Technology – Investigating Potatoes

FOCUS OBJECTIVES

- To develop observation skills
- To develop tactile exploration
- To encourage participation in group activities
- To develop listening skills
- To develop fine motor skills

EQUIPMENT

Selection of different kinds of potato – King Edward, sweet potato, Anya and new potatoes
Sheets of plain paper
Large sheet of card
Scissors
PVA glue/glue stick
Camera and film
Felt pens
Pencil
Knife and chopping board

METHOD

1. Pass around the selection of potatoes.
2. Feel the difference in shape and size.
3. Look at the colour and texture of their skins.
4. Draw around each kind of potato on a sheet of paper.
5. Write the name of the potato on each outline.
6. Colour in outlines.
7. Cut out each shape and glue on to a large piece of card.
8. Cut in half an example of each kind of potato.
9. Compare the different textures and colours of the inside of each potato.
10. Take photographs of each potato.
11. Add the photographs to the drawings on the poster.
12. Display poster with the potatoes.

Speechmark P This page may be photocopied for instructional use only. *Themed Activities for People with Learning Difficulties* © M Hutchinson 2003

RECORDING SHEET 3

THEME: TAKE A POTATO
Science & Technology – Investigating Potatoes

Name: ____________________ Date: ____________________

FOCUS OBJECTIVES	OBSERVATIONS AND COMMENTS
To develop observation skills	
To develop tactile exploration	
To encourage participation in group activities	
To develop listening skills	
To develop fine motor skills	

This page may be photocopied for instructional use only. *Themed Activities for People with Learning Difficulties* © M Hutchinson 2003

WORKSHEET 4

THEME: TAKE A POTATO
Community Living – Shopping

FOCUS OBJECTIVES

- To encourage recognition and matching skills
- To develop observation skills
- To develop literacy and numeracy skills
- To explore colour and shape
- To encourage tactile exploration

EQUIPMENT

Paper and pen
Pictures of shops – supermarket, DIY store, garden centre, greengrocer
Magazines, catalogues
Scissors
Glue stick
Purse/wallet and money
Transport

METHOD

1. Write a list of different kinds of potatoes.
2. Talk about which shops sell potatoes.
3. Find pictures of potatoes and the different kinds of shops.
4. Match the potatoes to the shops that sell them – for example King Edward – supermarket, seed potato – garden centre/DIY store.
5. Make a pictorial shopping list.
6. Look at the money in the purse/wallet – sort and match the coins and count them.
7. Decide what sort of potato is needed and how many.
8. Go to the appropriate shop.
9. Compare the prices of the potatoes.
10. Buy the potatoes.
11. Check change and add up the total amount of money spent.

Speechmark  This page may be photocopied for instructional use only. *Themed Activities for People with Learning Difficulties* © M Hutchinson 2003

RECORDING SHEET 4

THEME: TAKE A POTATO
Community Living – Shopping

Name: ______________________ Date: ______________________

FOCUS OBJECTIVES	OBSERVATIONS AND COMMENTS
To encourage recognition and matching skills	
To develop observation skills	
To develop literacy and numeracy skills	
To explore shape and colour	
To encourage tactile exploration	

This page may be photocopied for instructional use only. *Themed Activities for People with Learning Difficulties* © M Hutchinson 2003

ART & TEXTILES:
Greetings Card

- Fold a piece of card
- Draw a design or picture for front of card
- Cut out design
- Glue design to front of card
- Write message inside card
- Make an envelope
- Address envelope and put card inside

COMMUNICATION:
Make a Book

- Fold a piece of card in half
- Decide on the shape of the book – eg, rectangle, circle, square
- Draw chosen shape on to the folded card
- Choose what the book will be about – eg, cars, friends, animals
- Collect pictures about topic
- Put into book

Theme

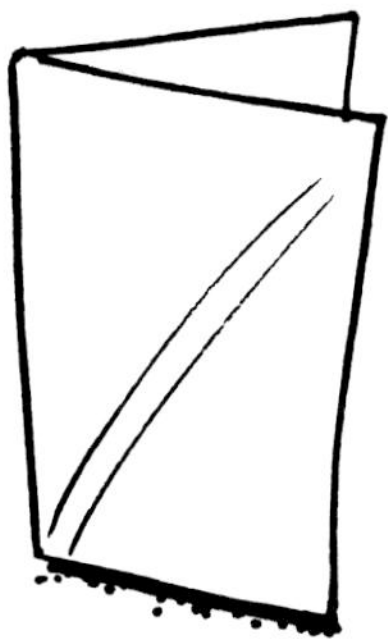

Take a piece of card

MEDIA STUDIES:
Create a Poster

- Choose a topic
- Research ideas using magazines and books
- Choose lettering
- Draw pictures or cut them out of magazines
- Position pictures and lettering on a large sheet of card
- Glue down
- Display poster

DRAMA:
Face Masks

- Look at faces
- Collect pictures of faces
- Draw outline of face and features on paper
- Colour in with paint, felt pens, etc
- Glue face on to card and trim
- Add hair
- Attach card handle to hold mask with

WORKSHEET 1

THEME: TAKE A PIECE OF CARD
Art & Textiles – Greetings Card

FOCUS OBJECTIVES

- To encourage self-expression
- To develop coordination skills
- To develop sequencing skills
- To practise literacy skills
- To have opportunities to make choices

EQUIPMENT

Card – selection of colours
Magazines, wrapping paper – for pictures and designs
Pencil, felt pens and colouring pencils
Scissors
PVA glue/glue stick
Paper – for envelope
Sticky tape
Ruler

METHOD

1. Fold a piece of card in half.
2. Look through magazines for pictures or designs and cut them out.
3. Make a drawing from one of the pictures.
4. Colour in the drawing.
5. Cut out drawing to fit the card.
6. Glue drawing or picture on to the front of the card.
7. Write a message on a separate piece of paper, to go inside the card.
8. Cut around the message and glue inside the card.
9. Alternatively, copy the message into the card.
10. Take a piece of paper to make an envelope. Measure it. It must be 5 cm (2 in) longer and 5 cm (2 in) wider than the piece of card before it was folded in half.
11. Measure 5 cm (2 in) down from the top of the paper. Mark with a pencil.
12. Fold the bottom edge of the paper up to the pencil mark.
13. Unfold the paper, and use the glue stick to seal the side edges of the envelope.
14. Slide the card in to the envelope, fold the top of the paper down and secure with a piece of tape.
15. Address the envelope.

Speechmark P This page may be photocopied for instructional use only. *Themed Activities for People with Learning Difficulties* © M Hutchinson 2003

RECORDING SHEET 1

THEME: TAKE A PIECE OF CARD
Art & Textiles – Greetings Card

Name: ______________________ Date: ______________________

FOCUS OBJECTIVES	OBSERVATIONS AND COMMENTS
To encourage self-expression	
To develop coordination skills	
To develop sequencing skills	
To practise literacy skills	
To have opportunities to make choices	

This page may be photocopied for instructional use only. *Themed Activities for People with Learning Difficulties* © M Hutchinson 2003

WORKSHEET 2

THEME: TAKE A PIECE OF CARD
Communication – Make a Book

FOCUS OBJECTIVES

- To develop literacy skills
- To encourage self-expression
- To develop listening skills
- To develop choice and decision-making
- To encourage participation in group activities

EQUIPMENT

Card – selection of colours
Books, magazines and photographs for ideas
Pencil, felt pens and colouring pencils
Scissors
Ruler
PVA glue/glue stick
Ribbon or string
Plain paper
Hole punch

METHOD

1 Fold a piece of card in half to make the cover of the book.
2 Decide on the shape of the book – rectangle, circle, triangle.
3 Draw the shape on to the folded card.
4 Cut out to make two identical shapes.
5 Choose what the book will be about. Collect pictures and photographs, and make drawings.
6 Use one of the card shapes as a template, and draw around it on several sheets of plain paper.
7 Glue the pictures and drawings, etc inside the shape drawn on the sheets of paper, and cut around the shape.
8 Decide on how many pages in the book.
9 Put the pages into the order you want them in, and place between the two pieces of card.
10 Punch holes in the left-hand side of the book.
11 Thread the ribbon or string through the holes, and tie loosely to allow the pages to turn.
12 Create a title and design for the cover of the book.
13 Make a group or individual book.

Speechmark P This page may be photocopied for instructional use only. *Themed Activities for People with Learning Difficulties* © M Hutchinson 2003

RECORDING SHEET 2

THEME: TAKE A PIECE OF CARD
Communication – Make a Book

Name: ______________________ Date: ______________________

FOCUS OBJECTIVES	OBSERVATIONS AND COMMENTS
To develop literacy skills	
To encourage self-expression	
To develop listening skills	
To develop choice and decision-making	
To encourage participation in group activities	

Speechmark This page may be photocopied for instructional use only. *Themed Activities for People with Learning Difficulties* © M Hutchinson 2003

WORKSHEET 3 | THEME: TAKE A PIECE OF CARD

Media Studies – Create a Poster

FOCUS OBJECTIVES

- To develop choice and decision-making
- To develop concentration span
- To encourage spatial awareness
- To develop sequencing skills
- To encourage participation in group activities

EQUIPMENT

Large piece of card
Books, magazines and photographs for ideas
Pencil, felt pens and colouring pencils
Scissors
PVA glue/glue stick
Ruler and pencil

METHOD

1. Choose a topic for the poster – for example, safety, food, transport.
2. Research ideas using magazines and books.
3. Draw pictures or cut them out of magazines.
4. Decide on the words needed in the poster.
5. Look through books and magazines at lettering used and choose a style for the poster.
6. Write the words for the poster in the lettering chosen.
7. Experiment with different colours.
8. Make a plan of the poster on a piece of paper.
9. Position the pictures and lettering on to the large piece of card.
10. Follow the plan of the poster.
11. Glue down the pictures and words.
12. Display the poster.

Speechmark P This page may be photocopied for instructional use only. *Themed Activities for People with Learning Difficulties* © M Hutchinson 2003

RECORDING SHEET 3

THEME: TAKE A PIECE OF CARD
Media Studies – Create a Poster

Name: ____________________ Date: ____________________

FOCUS OBJECTIVES	OBSERVATIONS AND COMMENTS
To develop choice and decision-making	
To develop concentration span	
To encourage spatial awareness	
To develop sequencing skills	
To encourage participation in group activities	

This page may be photocopied for instructional use only. *Themed Activities for People with Learning Difficulties* © M Hutchinson 2003

WORKSHEET 4

THEME: TAKE A PIECE OF CARD
Drama – Face Masks

FOCUS OBJECTIVES

- To encourage recognition and matching skills
- To develop hand-eye coordination
- To develop self-awareness
- To encourage peer group interaction
- To develop choice-making skills

EQUIPMENT

Card – selection of colours
Magazines
Pencil, felt pens, paints and coloured pencils
Scissors
PVA glue/glue stick
Wool – various colours
Sticky tape
Plain paper
Textured paper and material

METHOD

1. Look at faces – in magazines, photographs, in a mirror, other people.
2. Collect pictures of faces from magazines, etc.
3. Draw outline of face and features on a piece of paper.
4. Colour in features with paint, felt pens, coloured pencils, textured paper or material.
5. Glue face on to a piece of card and trim.
6. Add hair – use wool or shredded paper.
7. Attach a card handle to hold the mask with.
8. Sit in a circle.
9. Take turns to hold mask in front of face for the group to look at.
10. Make a series of masks that represent different emotions.
11. Use to explore how people are feeling.

Speechmark  This page may be photocopied for instructional use only. *Themed Activities for People with Learning Difficulties* © M Hutchinson 2003

RECORDING SHEET 4

THEME: TAKE A PIECE OF CARD
Drama – Face Masks

Name: ______________________ Date: ______________________

FOCUS OBJECTIVES	OBSERVATIONS AND COMMENTS
To encourage recognition and matching skills	
To develop hand-eye coordination	
To develop self-awareness	
To encourage peer group interaction	
To develop choice-making skills	

This page may be photocopied for instructional use only. *Themed Activities for People with Learning Difficulties* © M Hutchinson 2003

PHYSICAL EDUCATION:
Exercises

- Sit on chairs or mats in front of a mirror
- Point to self and others in mirror
- Nominate one person to begin exercise sequence
- Rest of group to watch in mirror and follow exercises
- Take turns in leading exercises

COMMUNICATION:
Building Relationships

- Sit side by side and opposite mirror
- Point to each of you in the mirror, to encourage eye-contact with the reflection
- Copy movement of person next to you
- Play gentle music
- Use ribbon-stick to exaggerate movement

Theme

Take a mirror

DRAMA:
Make-up

- Choose a character
- Use a table-top mirror
- Use moisturiser to cleanse skin
- Add make-up appropriate to chosen character
- Watch changes to face in mirror
- Brush hair or put on wig
- Practise character's expressions in front of mirror

ART & TEXTILES:
Mirror Printing

- Use ready-mix paints
- Pour different coloured paint on to a mirror-board or large mirror to create a pattern
- Lay a large piece of plain paper on top of paint
- Press down gently on paper
- Lift paper back to reveal print

WORKSHEET 1

THEME: TAKE A MIRROR
Physical Education – Exercises

FOCUS OBJECTIVES

- To develop awareness of self and others
- To develop coordination skills
- To develop sequencing skills
- To encourage turn-taking
- To develop listening skills

EQUIPMENT

Flip-chart or large piece of paper
Thick felt pen
Large mirror
Chairs or mats
List of exercises

METHOD

1. Make a list of exercises, for example – move head from side to side; lift up, then lower shoulders; shake hands; lift arms to shoulder height; lift arms above head; stretch arms as high as they will comfortably go; lower arms slowly; touch knees; touch toes; stamp feet.
2. Write the list on the flip-chart or large sheet of paper.
3. Position list where it can be seen easily.
4. Sit on chairs or mats in front of a large mirror.
5. Point to and name individuals' reflections in the mirror.
6. Ask each person in the group to point to themselves in the mirror.
7. Encourage individuals to point to named members of the group in the mirror.
8. Read through the exercises on the list.
9. Nominate one person to begin the exercise sequence.
10. Rest of the group to watch in the mirror and copy each exercise.
11. Repeat each exercise two or three times before moving on to the next one.
12. Take turns to lead the exercises.
13. Work through the exercises at the pace of the group.

Speechmark P This page may be photocopied for instructional use only. *Themed Activities for People with Learning Difficulties* © M Hutchinson 2003

RECORDING SHEET 1

THEME: TAKE A MIRROR
Physical Education – Exercises

Name: ______________________ Date: ______________________

FOCUS OBJECTIVES	OBSERVATIONS AND COMMENTS
To develop awareness of self and others	
To develop coordination skills	
To develop sequencing skills	
To encourage turn-taking	
To develop listening skills	

This page may be photocopied for instructional use only. *Themed Activities for People with Learning Difficulties* © M Hutchinson 2003

WORKSHEET 2 | THEME: TAKE A MIRROR

Communication – Building Relationships

FOCUS OBJECTIVES

- To develop awareness of self and others
- To encourage eye-contact
- To develop listening skills
- To develop visual tracking
- To work in a one-to-one situation

EQUIPMENT

Large mirror
Chairs
Tape recorder and gentle music
Torch
Ribbon-stick
Brightly coloured gloves

METHOD

1. Spend a short time sitting opposite each other.
2. Reach out and touch the hand of the person opposite.
3. Encourage eye-contact by introducing individuals or group members by name.
4. Work through some warm-up exercises together, for example – roll head from side to side; shrug shoulders; shake hands; breath in deeply and exhale.
5. Position chairs side by side and opposite the mirror.
6. Point to each person in the mirror.
7. Copy movements of another person to gain their attention.
8. Play gentle music and sway slowly from side to side.
9. Encourage individual movement to the music as well.
10. Wear brightly coloured gloves, and use a torch and a ribbon-stick to encourage eye-contact with reflected movements and images.

This page may be photocopied for instructional use only. *Themed Activities for People with Learning Difficulties* © M Hutchinson 2003

RECORDING SHEET 2

THEME: TAKE A MIRROR
Communication – Building Relationships

Name: ______________________ Date: ______________________

FOCUS OBJECTIVES	OBSERVATIONS AND COMMENTS
To develop awareness of self and others	
To encourage eye-contact	
To develop listening skills	
To develop visual tracking	
To work in a one-to-one situation	

This page may be photocopied for instructional use only. *Themed Activities for People with Learning Difficulties* © M Hutchinson 2003

WORKSHEET 3 | THEME: TAKE A MIRROR

Drama – Make-up

FOCUS OBJECTIVES

- To develop choice-making skills
- To develop concentration span
- To encourage tactile exploration
- To develop coordination skills
- To develop recognition of features

EQUIPMENT

Table-top mirror
Selection of make-up – theatrical, cosmetic, etc
Moisturiser
Cotton wool
Hairbrush
Wigs and hats
Pictures of different faces – clown, opera singer, animal, etc
Paper with outline of face and features on
Pen

METHOD

1. Look through pictures of faces.
2. Choose a character or style of make-up.
3. Write on an outline of a face any choices or preferences of make-up.
4. Look through the make-up and match the colours to those on the face plan.
5. Sit at the table in front of the mirror.
6. Point to the different features in the faces reflected.
7. Try naming them.
8. Use cotton wool and moisturiser to clean faces.
9. Begin to add the make-up – use the face plan for direction.
10. Watch in the mirror how the make-up changes how people look.
11. Brush hair or put on a wig or hat.
12. Choose a character and practise their expressions in the mirror.

This page may be photocopied for instructional use only. *Themed Activities for People with Learning Difficulties* © M Hutchinson 2003

RECORDING SHEET 3

THEME: TAKE A MIRROR
Drama – Make-up

Name: ________________ Date: ________________

FOCUS OBJECTIVES	OBSERVATIONS AND COMMENTS
To develop choice-making skills	
To develop concentration span	
To encourage tactile exploration	
To develop coordination skills	
To develop recognition of features	

This page may be photocopied for instructional use only. *Themed Activities for People with Learning Difficulties* © M Hutchinson 2003

WORKSHEET 4 | THEME: TAKE A MIRROR

Art & Textiles – Mirror Printing

FOCUS OBJECTIVES

- To encourage participation in group activities
- To develop spatial awareness
- To develop colour recognition and matching
- To develop fine motor skills
- To develop choice-making skills

EQUIPMENT

Large mirror or mirror-board
Newspaper
Selection of ready-mix paints
Small pots
Large pieces of plain paper
Aprons – one for each group member

METHOD

1. Cover the table with newspaper.
2. Position the mirror in the middle of the table.
3. Put on aprons and sit at the table.
4. Have the different colours of paint next to the mirror.
5. If the paints are not in plastic bottles that can be squeezed, pour small amounts into several small pots.
6. Pour different coloured paint on to the mirror.
7. Create an abstract pattern by overlapping the different colours of paint on the mirror.
8. Lay a large piece of plain paper on top of the paint.
9. Press down gently over the surface of the paper.
10. Lift one corner of the paper and gently peel it off the mirror to reveal the print.
11. Add more paint to the mirror for each additional print.
12. Make a collage from a selection of prints.

Speechmark  P This page may be photocopied for instructional use only. *Themed Activities for People with Learning Difficulties* © M Hutchinson 2003

RECORDING SHEET 4

THEME: TAKE A MIRROR
Art & Textiles – Mirror Printing

Name: ______________________ Date: ______________________

FOCUS OBJECTIVES	OBSERVATIONS AND COMMENTS
To encourage participation in group activities	
To develop spatial awareness	
To develop colour recognition and matching	
To develop fine motor skills	
To develop choice-making skills	

Speechmark This page may be photocopied for instructional use only. *Themed Activities for People with Learning Difficulties* © M Hutchinson 2003

COOKING:
Sponge Cake

- Find recipe
- Make a list of ingredients and equipment needed
- Collect together ingredients
- Prepare cooking area
- Make cake
- Decorate when cool, and serve

ART & TEXTILES:
Flour and Water Resist

- Mix flour with water to make a soft paste
- Draw a design on to a piece of white cotton material
- Cover design with the flour paste and dry
- Soak material in dye
- Wash out flour resist

Theme

Take a bag of flour

COMMUNITY LIVING:
Shopping Skills

- Find out what kind of flour and how much is needed to cook a cake
- Make a shopping list of ingredients
- Locate the flour in the shop
- Match the flour on the shelf with the flour on the list
- Pay for flour and other ingredients at checkout

THE ENVIRONMENT:
Origins of Flour

- Research topic – books, recipes, magazines
- Look at the history and geography of flour
- Make a poster about how flour is made
- List the different kinds of flour and their uses
- Draw a map of the world, and mark where wheat is grown

WORKSHEET 1

THEME: TAKE A BAG OF FLOUR
Cooking – Sponge Cake

FOCUS OBJECTIVES

- To develop sequencing skills
- To develop hand-eye coordination
- To experience a range of tastes, smells and textures
- To develop object recognition
- To develop an awareness of safety and hygiene

EQUIPMENT

Recipe for sponge cake
Ingredients – butter/margarine, castor sugar, eggs, self-raising flour, jam, icing sugar, etc
Mixing bowl
Cake tin
Oven gloves
Aprons – one for each group member
Cooling rack
Wooden spoon
Measuring scales
Plate

METHOD

1. Find a recipe for a sponge cake.
2. Make a list of ingredients and equipment needed.
3. Collect together all the ingredients.
4. Prepare the cooking area – wash the table, etc.
5. Look at each ingredient – feel it, smell it, taste it.
6. Weigh out the correct amounts of flour, sugar and butter or margarine.
7. Watch the textures of the ingredients change as they are mixed together.
8. Taste a small amount of the mixture before it goes into the cake tin.
9. While the cake is cooking, wash up and tidy away equipment.
10. Put away any unused ingredients.
11. Place the cooked cake on to a cooling rack.
12. When cool, sprinkle with icing sugar, cut and fill with jam.
13. Remember to use oven gloves when picking up hot items.

  This page may be photocopied for instructional use only. *Themed Activities for People with Learning Difficulties* © M Hutchinson 2003

RECORDING SHEET 1

THEME: TAKE A BAG OF FLOUR
Cooking – Sponge Cake

Name: ______________________ Date: ______________________

FOCUS OBJECTIVES	OBSERVATIONS AND COMMENTS
To develop sequencing skills	
To develop hand-eye coordination	
To experience a range of tastes, smells and textures	
To develop object recognition	
To develop an awareness of safety and hygiene	

This page may be photocopied for instructional use only. *Themed Activities for People with Learning Difficulties* © M Hutchinson 2003

Speechmark

WORKSHEET 2

THEME: TAKE A BAG OF FLOUR
Art & Textiles – Flour and Water Resist

FOCUS OBJECTIVES

- To encourage tactile exploration
- To encourage self-expression
- To develop listening skills
- To develop sequencing skills
- To encourage participation in group activities

EQUIPMENT

Flour
Water
Mixing bowl
Wooden spoon
Teaspoon
Aprons – one for each group member
White cotton material
Cold dye – blue, red, etc
Bucket
Microwave/oven
Newspaper

METHOD

1. Cover the table with newspaper.
2. Measure three cups of flour into the mixing bowl.
3. Mix with water, adding the water a little at a time.
4. Stop adding the water when the mixture is a soft, almost runny, paste.
5. Spread out material on the table.
6. Using a teaspoon, drop blobs of paste on to the material in a random pattern, or draw a pattern on the material and cover with paste.
7. Carefully transfer the material with the paste into an oven to dry.
8. Use a very low heat to avoid the paste or the material burning.
9. Check the material frequently and remove from the oven when dry.
10. Mix up the packet of dye – follow the instructions on the packet.
11. Add the material and leave to allow dye to transfer to material.
12. Dry material and iron on the reverse side to fix the dye.
13. Wash flour resist out of the material in cold water, and dry.
14. The material will be the colour of the dye, with white areas where the paste was.

This page may be photocopied for instructional use only. *Themed Activities for People with Learning Difficulties* © M Hutchinson 2003

Speechmark

RECORDING SHEET 2

THEME: TAKE A BAG OF FLOUR
Art & Textiles – Flour and Water Resist

Name: ______________________ Date: ______________________

FOCUS OBJECTIVES	OBSERVATIONS AND COMMENTS
To encourage tactile exploration	
To encourage self-expression	
To develop listening skills	
To develop sequencing skills	
To encourage participation in group activities	

This page may be photocopied for instructional use only. *Themed Activities for People with Learning Difficulties* © M Hutchinson 2003

WORKSHEET 3

THEME: TAKE A BAG OF FLOUR
Community Living – Shopping Skills

FOCUS OBJECTIVES

- To develop choice and decision-making
- To develop matching skills
- To work on literacy and numeracy skills
- To develop waiting skills
- To develop confidence in a variety of community-based venues

EQUIPMENT

Pen and paper
Recipe book
Pictures/photographs of a bag of flour
Purse/wallet with money
Transport

METHOD

Preparation for Trip

1. Look up a recipe for a sponge cake in the recipe book.
2. Find out what kind of flour and how much is needed to make the cake.
3. Include the information on the shopping list, along with the other ingredients. Use pictures and symbols as well as words.
4. Check the money in the purse/wallet is enough for the shopping.

Buying the Flour

1. Find a basket or trolley and locate the flour in the shop.
2. Match the flour on the shelf with the pictures/photographs on your shopping list, and select the correct type of flour.
3. Find the remaining ingredients, and put them in the basket or trolley.
4. Go to a checkout and transfer the ingredients on to the conveyor belt or counter.
5. Pay for the shopping and wait for the receipt and any change.

This page may be photocopied for instructional use only. *Themed Activities for People with Learning Difficulties* © M Hutchinson 2003

RECORDING SHEET 3

THEME: TAKE A BAG OF FLOUR
Community Living – Shopping Skills

Name: ______________________ Date: ______________________

FOCUS OBJECTIVES	OBSERVATIONS AND COMMENTS
To develop choice and decision-making	
To develop matching skills	
To work on literacy and numeracy skills	
To develop waiting skills	
To develop confidence in a variety of community-based venues	

This page may be photocopied for instructional use only. *Themed Activities for People with Learning Difficulties* © M Hutchinson 2003

WORKSHEET 4

THEME: TAKE A BAG OF FLOUR
The Environment – Origins of Flour

FOCUS OBJECTIVES

- To develop research techniques
- To encourage participation in group activities
- To develop fine motor skills
- To encourage self-expression
- To develop matching skills

EQUIPMENT

Card – selection of colours
Magazines
Pencil, felt pens, paints and colouring pencils
Scissors
PVA glue/glue stick
Plain paper
Books – plants, cooking, industry, etc
Atlas
Empty flour bags
Small see-through bags

METHOD

1 Look through magazines and cut out any pictures connected with flour.
2 Look at the history and geography of flour – for example which plant it comes from, where that plant grows.
3 Draw a map of the world and mark on it where wheat is grown.
4 Look at how flour is made.
5 Make a poster with the information collected.
6 List the different types of flour and their uses – present your information either as another poster or in a scrapbook.
7 Collect samples of different kinds of flour and seal in small see-through bags.
8 Attach the bags to a large sheet of card and label them.
9 Display posters and scrapbook for others to see.

Speechmark P This page may be photocopied for instructional use only. *Themed Activities for People with Learning Difficulties* © M Hutchinson 2003

RECORDING SHEET 4

THEME: TAKE A BAG OF FLOUR
The Environment – Origins of Flour

Name: ______________________ Date: ______________________

FOCUS OBJECTIVES	OBSERVATIONS AND COMMENTS
To develop research techniques	
To encourage participation in group activities	
To develop fine motor skills	
To encourage self-expression	
To develop matching skills	

This page may be photocopied for instructional use only. *Themed Activities for People with Learning Difficulties* © M Hutchinson 2003

SCIENCE & TECHNOLOGY:
Experiments with Paper

- Make a list of different kinds of paper – eg, tissue paper, tracing paper, cartridge paper
- Collect the different kinds of paper
- Test each kind of paper for absorbency, folding, how much light it lets through, how easy it is to tear, etc

COMMUNITY LIVING:
Presenting a Menu

- Select food for menu
- Choose lettering
- Write on a piece of paper
- Find pictures of food linked to the menu
- Cut out
- Position pictures on menu and glue on
- Laminate menu or put into a plastic wallet

Theme

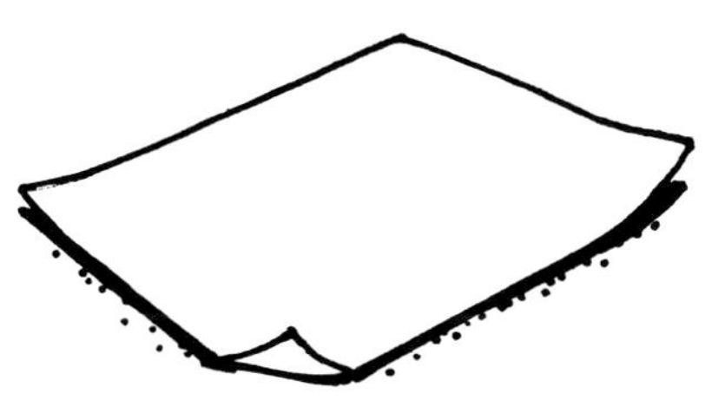

Take a piece of paper

COMMUNICATION:
Newsletter

- Pick topics to report about
- Interview people
- Record interviews using words, photographs, pictures, symbols and a tape recorder
- Use information to decide on page layout
- Position information on a sheet of paper and glue
- Make copies of newsletter

ART & TEXTILES:
Looking at Colour

- Choose 2 or 3 different colours of tissue paper
- Tear into irregular shapes
- Spread the glue evenly over the tray
- Cover glue with different coloured pieces of tissue paper
- Add more glue and tissue paper – about 3 layers – and leave to dry
- Peel off tray and trim

WORKSHEET 1

THEME: TAKE A PIECE OF PAPER
Science & Technology – Experiments with Paper

FOCUS OBJECTIVES

- To develop an understanding of cause and effect
- To develop coordination skills
- To encourage tactile exploration
- To develop listening skills
- To encourage observation skills

EQUIPMENT

Selection of different kinds of paper – tissue, tracing, blotting, cartridge, rice paper, etc
Jug of water and a shallow tray
Torch
Large sheets of paper
Thick felt pens
Large piece of card
Scissors
PVA glue/glue stick

METHOD

1. Make a list of different kinds of paper.
2. Collect as many kinds of paper from the list as you can.
3. Cut a small piece of each kind of paper and glue on to the piece of card.
4. Feel the texture of each kind of paper – use fingertips, palms and the side of your face.
5. Label each piece of paper.
6. Test each kind of paper for absorbency – pour a small amount of water into the shallow tray and, one at a time, drop a piece of paper on to the water.
7. Watch what happens to the paper and record your findings.
8. Repeat the procedure, but test the paper for how much light is let through; how strong it is; how easy it is to fold; how easy it is to tear; and how quickly it falls to the floor when dropped.
9. Make bar graphs out of the information collected.
10. Make a display about the experiments and the results.
11. Provide examples of the paper tested for others to feel.

Speechmark P This page may be photocopied for instructional use only. *Themed Activities for People with Learning Difficulties* © M Hutchinson 2003

RECORDING SHEET 1

THEME: TAKE A PIECE OF PAPER
Science & Technology – Experiments with Paper

Name: ______________________ Date: ______________

FOCUS OBJECTIVES	OBSERVATIONS AND COMMENTS
To develop an understanding of cause and effect	
To develop coordination skills	
To encourage tactile exploration	
To develop listening skills	
To encourage observation skills	

This page may be photocopied for instructional use only. *Themed Activities for People with Learning Difficulties* © M Hutchinson 2003

Speechmark

WORKSHEET 2

THEME: TAKE A PIECE OF PAPER
Community Living – Presenting a Menu

FOCUS OBJECTIVES

- To develop awareness of self and others
- To develop choice and decision-making
- To encourage self-expression
- To develop literacy skills
- To develop matching skills

EQUIPMENT

Recipe books
Magazines/photographs – for pictures of food
Examples of menus – restaurants/fast food chains, etc
Scissors
PVA glue/glue stick
Sheets of plain paper – assorted colours
Plastic wallets or laminating machine
Felt pens
Ruler

METHOD

1. Talk about what a menu is for.
2. Discuss what a healthy diet should include.
3. Look through recipe books and select food and dishes for the menu.
4. Make a list of the chosen dishes.
5. Choose the lettering – use felt pens, typewriter or computer.
6. Write or print the menu on a piece of A4 paper – any colour.
7. Find pictures of food linked with the menu.
8. Cut out and position around the writing on the menu.
9. When the pictures are in the right positions, glue down.
10. Laminate the menu, or put into a plastic wallet.

Speechmark P This page may be photocopied for instructional use only. *Themed Activities for People with Learning Difficulties* © M Hutchinson 2003

RECORDING SHEET 2

THEME: TAKE A PIECE OF PAPER
Community Living – Presenting a Menu

Name: ______________________ Date: ______________________

FOCUS OBJECTIVES	OBSERVATIONS AND COMMENTS
To develop awareness of self and others	
To develop choice and decision-making	
To encourage self-expression	
To develop literacy skills	
To develop matching skills	

  This page may be photocopied for instructional use only. *Themed Activities for People with Learning Difficulties* © M Hutchinson 2003

WORKSHEET 3

THEME: TAKE A PIECE OF PAPER
Communication – Newsletter

FOCUS OBJECTIVES

- To develop choice and decision-making
- To develop literacy skills
- To encourage participation in group activities
- To develop listening skills
- To encourage self-expression

EQUIPMENT

Sheets of paper and pen
Tape recorder and blank tape
Camera and film
PVA glue/glue stick
A newspaper/magazine
Large sheet of plain paper and thick felt pen

METHOD

1. Make a list of topics to report on – eg, pets people have, hobbies, favourite television programmes, fashion, etc.
2. Write down the names of people to be interviewed.
3. Contact them to arrange a time for an interview.
4. Look through a newspaper or magazine for ideas of what to include in an article and the layout of a page.
5. Practise using the tape recorder with members of the group – ask each person to vocalise or say their name, and play back the recording.
6. Write down some questions to ask during the interviews – use pictures and objects as well as words.
7. Complete the interviews.
8. Take photographs.
9. Collect together all the information, and use it to work out the page layout.
10. Position the writing and photographs on a sheet of paper and glue down.
11. Make copies of the newsletter and circulate.

Speechmark  This page may be photocopied for instructional use only. *Themed Activities for People with Learning Difficulties* © M Hutchinson 2003

RECORDING SHEET 3

THEME: TAKE A PIECE OF PAPER
Communication – Newsletter

Name: ______________________ Date: ______________________

FOCUS OBJECTIVES	OBSERVATIONS AND COMMENTS
To develop choice and decision-making	
To develop literacy skills	
To encourage participation in group activities	
To develop listening skills	
To encourage self-expression	

 This page may be photocopied for instructional use only. *Themed Activities for People with Learning Difficulties* © M Hutchinson 2003

WORKSHEET 4

THEME: TAKE A PIECE OF PAPER
Art & Textiles – Looking at Colour

FOCUS OBJECTIVES

- To encourage participation in group activities
- To develop spatial awareness
- To develop colour recognition and matching
- To develop fine motor skills
- To develop choice-making skills

EQUIPMENT

Small tray
Newspaper
Selection of different coloured tissue paper
PVA glue in a small pot
Paintbrush
Large plastic bag – with no writing on
Aprons – one for each group member

METHOD

1. Cover the table with newspaper.
2. Choose 2 or 3 different colours of tissue paper.
3. Tear the tissue paper into irregular shapes, and put to one side of the table.
4. Cut the plastic bag to the size of the tray.
5. Place the plastic bag on the tray.
6. Pour a large blob of glue on the plastic bag.
7. Spread the glue evenly over the bag, using the paintbrush.
8. Cover the glue with the tissue paper shapes – overlap the pieces of paper.
9. Brush another layer of glue on to the tissue paper, and add another layer of tissue paper.
10. Repeat this again and allow to dry.
11. Peel the tissue paper layers off the tray, and separate from the plastic bag.
12. Trim and hang in a window.

Speechmark  This page may be photocopied for instructional use only. *Themed Activities for People with Learning Difficulties* © M Hutchinson 2003

RECORDING SHEET 4

THEME: TAKE A PIECE OF PAPER
Art & Textiles – Looking at Colour

Name: ______________________ Date: ______________

FOCUS OBJECTIVES	OBSERVATIONS AND COMMENTS
To encourage participation in group activities	
To develop spatial awareness	
To develop colour recognition and matching	
To develop fine motor skills	
To develop choice-making skills	

This page may be photocopied for instructional use only. *Themed Activities for People with Learning Difficulties* © M Hutchinson 2003

Speechmark

ART & TEXTILES:
Branch Weaving

- Find a fallen branch
- Decorate a large pot
- Secure branch in the large pot – weight pot with soil/sand/clay, etc
- Weave lengths of wool, ribbon, strips of paper, etc in and out of twigs on branch
- Trim untidy ends with scissors

THE ENVIRONMENT:
Seasons

- Research the seasons
- Look at trees during each season – buds, blossom, fruit, leaves, no leaves, etc
- Make a poster of trees, using photographs, pictures and drawings
- Use a fallen winter branch to make models of branches in each season

Theme

Take a branch

COMMUNICATION:
Family/Group Tree

- Select a fallen branch
- Secure it in a pot
- Take photographs of family or group members
- Cut out each person – head and shoulders – from photographs
- Glue on to card and trim
- Punch a hole in top of photograph
- Attach to branch with cotton or wool

PHYSICAL EDUCATION:
Collecting Branches

- Wear sensible shoes and clothes
- Choose a park or open space that has trees
- Find out about different kinds of trees
- Look around the base of trees
- Select fallen branches
- Put into large bag

WORKSHEET 1

THEME: TAKE A BRANCH
Art & Textiles – Branch Weaving

FOCUS OBJECTIVES

- To encourage tactile exploration
- To develop hand-eye coordination
- To develop spatial awareness
- To develop concentration span
- To have opportunities to make choices

EQUIPMENT

Newspaper
A fallen branch
Large pot
Clay, soil, sand to secure branch in pot
Wool, ribbon, strips of material/paper, etc
Scissors
Ready-mix paint and brush
PVA glue

METHOD

1. Cover the table with newspaper.
2. Decorate the pot with the paint.
3. When the paint has dried, cover it with a coat of PVA glue.
4. Fill the pot with the sand or soil – about three-quarters full.
5. Clay may be used as an alternative, by making a ball shape about the size of a small melon, and pushing it firmly into the bottom of the pot.
6. Secure the branch in the pot by pushing it into the sand, soil or clay.
7. Decide whether or not to paint the branch.
8. Cut long lengths of ribbon, wool and material.
9. Choose a piece and weave it in and out of the twigs on the branch.
10. Continue to add wool and ribbon to the branch with a selection of colours and materials.
11. Trim any untidy ends with the scissors.
12. Display the decorated branch.

This page may be photocopied for instructional use only. *Themed Activities for People with Learning Difficulties* © M Hutchinson 2003
Speechmark

RECORDING SHEET 1

THEME: TAKE A BRANCH
Art & Textiles – Branch Weaving

Name: ______________________ Date: ______________________

FOCUS OBJECTIVES	OBSERVATIONS AND COMMENTS
To encourage tactile exploration	
To develop hand-eye coordination	
To develop spatial awareness	
To have opportunities to make choices	

This page may be photocopied for instructional use only. *Themed Activities for People with Learning Difficulties* © M Hutchinson 2003

WORKSHEET 2

THEME: TAKE A BRANCH
The Environment – Seasons

FOCUS OBJECTIVES

- To develop observation skills
- To encourage tactile exploration
- To develop environmental awareness
- To develop sequencing skills
- To encourage participation in group activities

EQUIPMENT

Several small fallen branches without leaves on
Books, magazines and pictures of the seasons and trees
Tissue paper – pink, white, green, brown, red, orange
Large piece of card
Scissors
PVA glue/glue stick

METHOD

1. Research the seasons – look through books and magazines for pictures of trees during each season.
2. Look at trees during each season – with buds, blossom, fruit, leaves, no leaves, etc.
3. Make a poster of trees through the year, using photographs, pictures and drawings.
4. From the information collected, make a model of a tree in each season using four fallen branches.
5. Spring – use pink and white tissue paper for blossom.
6. Summer – use green tissue paper for leaves and red for fruit.
7. Autumn – use brown and orange tissue paper for leaves.
8. Winter – use a plain branch.
9. Label each branch.
10. Display the branches with the poster.

Speechmark P This page may be photocopied for instructional use only. *Themed Activities for People with Learning Difficulties* © M Hutchinson 2003

RECORDING SHEET 2

THEME: TAKE A BRANCH
The Environment – Seasons

Name: ______________________ Date: ______________________

FOCUS OBJECTIVES	OBSERVATIONS AND COMMENTS
To develop observation skills	
To encourage tactile exploration	
To develop environmental awareness	
To develop sequencing skills	
To encourage participation in group activities	

This page may be photocopied for instructional use only. *Themed Activities for People with Learning Difficulties* © M Hutchinson 2003

WORKSHEET 3

THEME: TAKE A BRANCH
Communication – Family/Group Tree

FOCUS OBJECTIVES

- To develop observation skills
- To develop choice and decision-making skills
- To encourage awareness of self and others
- To develop listening skills
- To encourage participation in group activities

EQUIPMENT

Large pot to put branch in
Branch – with no leaves on
Camera and film
Self-adhesive labels
Felt pens
Scissors
Hole punch
Glue stick
Sheets of card
Wool or ribbon

METHOD

1. Select a fallen branch and secure it in a large pot.
2. Take two photographs of each member in the group.
3. Have the film developed and printed.
4. Ask each person to choose their favourite photograph out of the two prints.
5. Cut around the head and shoulders of each person's selected photograph.
6. Glue on to a piece of card, and trim to make a border.
7. Punch a hole in the top of the mounted photograph.
8. Thread the wool or ribbon through the hole and tie in a loop.
9. Write names on self-adhesive labels and match names to photographs.
10. Ask each person to hang their own photograph on the 'tree', or to indicate where to hang it by pointing or saying.

Speechmark  This page may be photocopied for instructional use only. *Themed Activities for People with Learning Difficulties* © M Hutchinson 2003

RECORDING SHEET 3

THEME: TAKE A BRANCH
Communication – Family/Group Tree

Name: ______________________ Date: ______________

FOCUS OBJECTIVES	OBSERVATIONS AND COMMENTS
To develop observation skills	
To develop choice and decision-making skills	
To encourage awareness of self and others	
To develop listening skills	
To encourage participation in group activities	

This page may be photocopied for instructional use only. *Themed Activities for People with Learning Difficulties* © M Hutchinson 2003

WORKSHEET 4

THEME: TAKE A BRANCH

Physical Education – Collecting Branches

FOCUS OBJECTIVES

- To encourage recognition and matching skills
- To develop observation skills
- To develop environmental awareness
- To develop mobility skills
- To encourage tactile exploration

EQUIPMENT

Sensible footwear and clothes
Transport – if required
A park or open space
Large bag
Pictures of trees and branches – books and magazines
Plastic wallets
Sheets of plain paper and crayons

METHOD

1. Look at pictures of trees and branches.
2. Cut pictures out of gardening magazines – put into a plastic wallet to take on outing.
3. Talk about the venue and where it is.
4. Put on shoes or boots and coats.
5. At the park or open space look at the trees.
6. Feel the bark on different trees.
7. Look around the base of the trees for fallen branches.
8. Select branches that have interesting shapes and textures.
9. Put the selected branches into the large bag.
10. Take bark rubbings of some of the trees in the park, using paper and crayons.
11. Put the bark rubbings into a plastic folder.
12. Make a display out of the branches collected and the bark rubbings taken.
13. Match the bark rubbings to the branches from the same trees.

Speechmark  P This page may be photocopied for instructional use only. *Themed Activities for People with Learning Difficulties* © M Hutchinson 2003

RECORDING SHEET 4

THEME: TAKE A BRANCH
Physical Education – Collecting Branches

Name: ______________________ Date: ______________________

FOCUS OBJECTIVES	OBSERVATIONS AND COMMENTS
To encourage recognition and matching skills	
To develop observation skills	
To develop environmental awareness	
To develop mobility skills	
To encourage tactile exploration	

This page may be photocopied for instructional use only. *Themed Activities for People with Learning Difficulties* © M Hutchinson 2003

THE ENVIRONMENT:
Bottle Garden

- Cut top off a 2-litre plastic bottle
- Fill half-full with compost
- Drop seeds into bottle
- Cover seeds with thin layer of compost
- Water
- Put in a warm and light place
- Water as plants grow

SCIENCE & TECHNOLOGY:
Looking at Soil

- Rinse out a 2-litre plastic bottle
- Collect some soil
- Spoon soil in through a funnel
- Fill bottle three-quarters full of water
- Secure lid and shake bottle
- Leave to settle

Theme

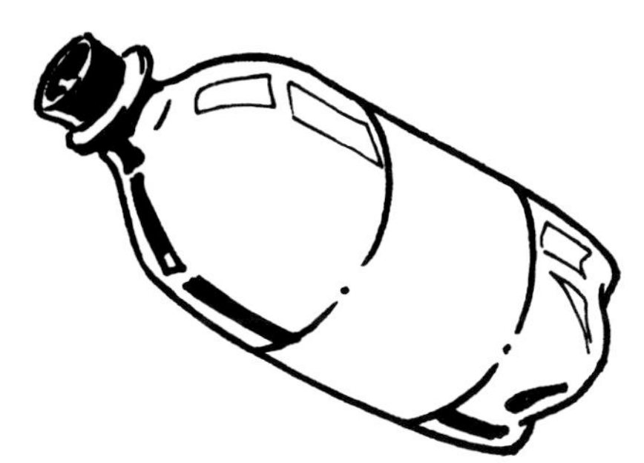

Take a plastic bottle

MUSIC:
Auditory Bottles

- Rinse and dry a 2-litre plastic bottle
- Fill with a cup of dried peas
- Screw on lid and secure with tape
- Decorate outside of bottle
- Repeat process with more bottles, using sand, lentils, metal washers, etc
- Listen to difference in sounds

ART & TEXTILES:
Sensory Bottles

- Rinse and dry a 2-litre plastic bottle
- Remove label
- Tie a selection of beads, ribbons, shiny paper, etc together
- Suspend from top of bottle with cotton
- Screw on lid, secure with tape
- Shine a torch through bottle

WORKSHEET 1

THEME: TAKE A PLASTIC BOTTLE
The Environment – Bottle Garden

FOCUS OBJECTIVES

- To develop an understanding of cause and effect
- To develop fine motor skills
- To develop sequencing skills
- To encourage sensory exploration
- To develop observation skills

EQUIPMENT

Clear plastic 2-litre bottles
Compost
Craft knife
Seeds, various small plants
Tablespoon or small trowel
Aprons – one for each group member
Newspaper
Watering-can
Self-adhesive labels and pen

METHOD

1. Cover the table with newspaper.
2. Rinse out the bottles and drain.
3. Carefully cut the bottles in half with the craft knife.
4. Stand the bottom section of the bottles on the table.
5. Fill the bottles half full of compost.
6. Open a packet of seeds.
7. Drop about 10 seeds into one of the bottle bottoms.
8. Cover the seeds with a thin layer of compost.
9. Water.
10. Write the name of the seeds and the date on a self-adhesive label and stick it to the bottle.
11. Put other seeds or plants into the other bottles.
12. Place the bottle garden in a warm and light place.
13. Water as the plants grow.

This page may be photocopied for instructional use only. *Themed Activities for People with Learning Difficulties* © M Hutchinson 2003

RECORDING SHEET 1

THEME: TAKE A PLASTIC BOTTLE
The Environment – Bottle Garden

Name: ______________________ Date: ______________________

FOCUS OBJECTIVES	OBSERVATIONS AND COMMENTS
To develop an understanding of cause and effect	
To develop fine motor skills	
To develop sequencing skills	
To encourage sensory exploration	
To develop observation skills	

This page may be photocopied for instructional use only. *Themed Activities for People with Learning Difficulties* © M Hutchinson 2003

WORKSHEET 2

THEME: TAKE A PLASTIC BOTTLE
Science & Technology – Looking at Soil

FOCUS OBJECTIVES

- To develop observation skills
- To encourage tactile and visual exploration
- To develop an understanding of cause and effect
- To encourage participation in group activities
- To develop environmental awareness

EQUIPMENT

Clear plastic 2-litre bottles
Soil
Bags to put soil in
Trowel or tablespoon
Sheets of paper
Newspaper
Aprons – one for each group member
Self-adhesive labels and pen

METHOD

1 Rinse out the plastic bottles and drain.
2 Collect soil from different locations – garden, park.
3 Make a paper funnel from a sheet of paper.
4 Put the funnel into the top of one bottle.
5 Spoon small amounts of soil, from one bag, into the funnel.
6 Fill the bottle about a quarter full with soil.
7 Fill the bottle three-quarters full of water.
8 Put on the lid tightly.
9 Shake the bottle vigorously.
10 Repeat steps 4–9 with the other bottle.
10 Stand the bottles on the table and leave the soil to settle.
11 The soil will settle into different layers.
12 Make a label for each bottle to say where the soil came from.
13 Compare the different samples of soil when they have all settled.

  This page may be photocopied for instructional use only. *Themed Activities for People with Learning Difficulties* © M Hutchinson 2003

RECORDING SHEET 2

THEME: TAKE A PLASTIC BOTTLE
Science & Technology – Looking at Soil

Name: Date:

FOCUS OBJECTIVES	OBSERVATIONS AND COMMENTS
To develop observation skills	
To encourage tactile and visual exploration	
To develop an understanding of cause and effect	
To encourage participation in group activities	
To develop environmental awareness	

This page may be photocopied for instructional use only. *Themed Activities for People with Learning Difficulties* © M Hutchinson 2003

WORKSHEET 3

THEME: TAKE A PLASTIC BOTTLE
Music – Auditory Bottles

FOCUS OBJECTIVES

- To develop choice-making skills
- To develop listening skills
- To encourage tactile exploration
- To develop coordination skills
- To develop anticipation

EQUIPMENT

Clear plastic 2-litre bottles
Dried peas, lentils, sand, gravel, metal washers, etc
Brightly coloured paper, material, ribbon
Scissors
Glue stick
Sticky tape
Plastic funnel
Small pot or bowls

METHOD

1. Rinse and dry the bottles.
2. Place the dried peas, lentils, etc into small pots or bowls.
3. Explore the texture and sound of the dried peas by touching them, holding them and dropping them back into the container.
4. Repeat this with the contents of each container.
5. Place the funnel into the top of a bottle and tip in the dried peas.
6. Screw the lid back on.
7. Decorate the outside of the bottle with paper or material.
8. Repeat the process for each bottle.
9. When all the bottles are complete, spend time holding and shaking each bottle.
10. Listen to the different sounds they make.

Speechmark  P This page may be photocopied for instructional use only. *Themed Activities for People with Learning Difficulties* © M Hutchinson 2003

RECORDING SHEET 3

THEME: TAKE A PLASTIC BOTTLE
Music – Auditory Bottles

Name: ______________________ Date: ______________

FOCUS OBJECTIVES	OBSERVATIONS AND COMMENTS
To develop choice-making skills	
To develop listening skills	
To encourage tactile exploration	
To develop coordination skills	
To develop anticipation	

This page may be photocopied for instructional use only. *Themed Activities for People with Learning Difficulties* © M Hutchinson 2003

WORKSHEET 4

THEME: TAKE A PLASTIC BOTTLE
Art & Textiles – Sensory Bottles

FOCUS OBJECTIVES

- To develop visual exploration and tracking
- To develop concentration span
- To encourage participation in activities
- To develop fine motor skills
- To develop choice-making skills

EQUIPMENT

Plastic 2-litre bottles – clear, green, orange
Beads, ribbon, reflective materials
Wool or thread
Scissors
Tape
Torch

METHOD

1 Rinse and dry a 2-litre clear plastic bottle.
2 Remove the label.
3 Explore the selection of materials through touch and sight.
4 Choose any items that are of particular interest.
5 Tie together the chosen items with wool or thread.
6 Feed into the bottle, and suspend by winding the thread around the neck of the bottle.
7 Screw the lid back on and secure with tape.
8 Repeat the process with other bottles.
9 Use a torch to shine through the bottles.
10 Twist, tip or roll the bottles to move the contents around.
11 Smaller bottles can also be used.

Speechmark  This page may be photocopied for instructional use only. *Themed Activities for People with Learning Difficulties* © M Hutchinson 2003

RECORDING SHEET 4

THEME: TAKE A PLASTIC BOTTLE
Art & Textiles – Sensory Bottles

Name:

Date:

FOCUS OBJECTIVES	OBSERVATIONS AND COMMENTS
To develop visual exploration and tracking	
To develop concentration span	
To encourage participation in activities	
To develop fine motor skills	
To develop choice-making skills	

This page may be photocopied for instructional use only. *Themed Activities for People with Learning Difficulties* © M Hutchinson 2003

COMMUNICATION:
Basic Numeracy

- Buy a large bag of assorted balloons
- Sort balloons into colours
- Record findings on a chart
- Sort balloons into shapes
- Record findings on a chart
- Count how many colours and shapes there are in the bag

ART & TEXTILES:
Paint Bombs

- Mix selection of different coloured paints
- Fill balloons with the paint
- Spread a very large piece of paper on the floor
- Throw the paint bombs on to the paper
- Allow picture to dry

Theme

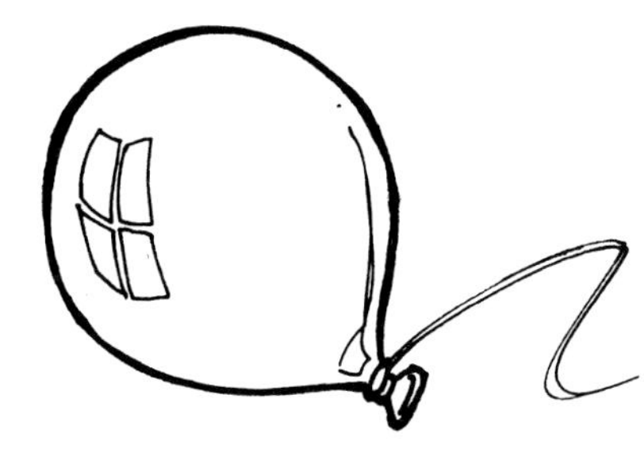

Take a balloon

SCIENCE & TECHNOLOGY:
Balloon Experiments

- Look at and feel a deflated balloon
- Blow up balloon, then let it go
- Blow up balloon, tie end – look at and feel balloon
- Throw balloon up in the air and watch it fall
- Burst balloon

INTERACTIVE GROUP GAMES:
Table Balloon Tennis

- Sit at opposite ends of a table
- Use tape on the table to mark out net
- Blow up balloon and tie end
- Hit balloon across table to opponent
- Play in pairs/teams of two

WORKSHEET 1

THEME: TAKE A BALLOON
Communication – Basic Numeracy

FOCUS OBJECTIVES

- To develop colour and shape recognition
- To develop fine motor skills
- To develop numeracy skills
- To encourage turn-taking
- To develop listening skills

EQUIPMENT

Flip-chart or large pieces of paper
Thick felt pens – different colours
Bag of assorted balloons

METHOD

1. Open the bag of balloons.
2. Tip the balloons out of the bag on to the table.
3. Sort the balloons into colours.
4. Write each colour on the flip-chart or large sheet of paper – use the same colour felt pen.
5. Sort the balloons into shapes.
6. Draw the different shapes on another large sheet of paper.
7. Count how many balloons are the same colour and shape.
8. Make a chart to show your results – draw small balloon shapes, cut them out and colour in.
9. Glue on to a sheet of paper, for example three blue round balloons, two yellow long balloons, etc.
10. Blow up a few balloons of different shapes to see how they change in size.
11. Make a display of all the information collected.

P This page may be photocopied for instructional use only. *Themed Activities for People with Learning Difficulties* © M Hutchinson 2003

RECORDING SHEET 1

THEME: TAKE A BALLOON
Communication – Basic Numeracy

Name: ______________________ Date: ______________________

FOCUS OBJECTIVES	OBSERVATIONS AND COMMENTS
To develop colour and shape recognition	
To develop fine motor skills	
To develop numeracy skills	
To encourage turn-taking	
To develop listening skills	

This page may be photocopied for instructional use only. *Themed Activities for People with Learning Difficulties* © M Hutchinson 2003

WORKSHEET 2 | THEME: TAKE A BALLOON
Art & Textiles – Paint Bombs

FOCUS OBJECTIVES

- To develop colour matching
- To encourage eye-contact
- To develop listening skills
- To develop an understanding of cause and effect
- To encourage participation in group activities

EQUIPMENT

Paint – ready-mix in selection of colours
Bag of balloons
Very large piece of paper – eg, white paper table-cloth
Aprons – one for each group member
Masking tape
Jug
Funnel
Washing-up bowl/bucket

METHOD

1. Mix the red paint to a runny consistency.
2. Pour into a jug.
3. Find a red balloon.
4. Put the funnel into the opening of the balloon.
5. Carefully pour the paint into the balloon – only half fill.
6. Take out the funnel and tie a knot in the balloon.
7. Put the balloon in a washing-up bowl or bucket.
8. Repeat the process with the other colours that you have chosen.
9. Take the large sheet of paper outside and secure it to the ground or a wall with the masking tape.
10. Drop or throw the paint-filled balloons on to the sheet of paper – hard enough to burst the balloons.
11. Allow the pattern created by the paint bombs to dry.
12. Trim and display.

Speechmark  This page may be photocopied for instructional use only. *Themed Activities for People with Learning Difficulties* © M Hutchinson 2003

RECORDING SHEET 2

THEME: TAKE A BALLOON
Art & Textiles – Paint Bombs

Name: ______________________ Date: ______________________

FOCUS OBJECTIVES	OBSERVATIONS AND COMMENTS
To develop colour matching	
To encourage eye-contact	
To develop listening skills	
To develop an understanding of cause and effect	
To encourage participation in group activities	

Speechmark P This page may be photocopied for instructional use only. *Themed Activities for People with Learning Difficulties* © M Hutchinson 2003

WORKSHEET 3

THEME: TAKE A BALLOON
Science & Technology – Balloon Experiments

FOCUS OBJECTIVES

- To develop an understanding of cause and effect
- To develop observation skills
- To encourage tactile exploration
- To develop hand-eye coordination
- To develop auditory and visual tracking

EQUIPMENT

Bag of balloons
Bag of dried peas
Safety pin

METHOD

1. Open the bag of balloons.
2. Take out 3 or 4 balloons.
3. Look at and feel a deflated balloon – scrunch it and stretch it.
4. Blow up a balloon – then let it go and see how far it travels.
5. Blow up another balloon – let the air out of it to make a noise.
6. Blow up a balloon, tie the end – look at it and feel it.
7. Throw the balloon into the air and watch it fall.
8. Fill a balloon with a small amount of dried peas, blow it up and tie the end.
9. Shake the balloon to move the dried peas around inside.
10. Drop the filled balloon and watch it fall.
11. Try different 'fillings' – for example water, sand, lentils, etc.
12. Drop an unfilled balloon at the same time as a filled balloon, and compare how they fall.
13. Use a safety pin to burst an unfilled balloon, or stamp on one. This is best left to the end of the activity as it may unsettle some individuals.

Speechmark  This page may be photocopied for instructional use only. *Themed Activities for People with Learning Difficulties* © M Hutchinson 2003

RECORDING SHEET 3

THEME: TAKE A BALLOON
Science & Technology – Balloon Experiments

Name: ______________________ Date: ______________________

FOCUS OBJECTIVES	OBSERVATIONS AND COMMENTS
To develop an understanding of cause and effect	
To develop observation skills	
To encourage tactile exploration	
To develop hand-eye coordination	
To develop auditory and visual tracking	

WORKSHEET 4

THEME: TAKE A BALLOON
Interactive Group Games – Table Balloon Tennis

FOCUS OBJECTIVES

- To encourage participation in group activities
- To develop spatial awareness
- To develop numeracy skills
- To develop hand-eye coordination
- To develop turn-taking skills

EQUIPMENT

Table and 4 chairs
Masking tape
Bag of balloons
Large sheet of paper and thick felt pen
Cassette player
Fast instrumental music on cassette

METHOD

1. Position two chairs at one end of the table, and two at the opposite end – have the table lengthways to the chairs.
2. Find the middle of the table and mark out the 'net' with a double line of masking tape.
3. Blow up several balloons.
4. Choose team names.
5. Write the team names on a large sheet of paper to make a score board.
6. Agree on a scoring system before you start a game.
7. Toss a coin to see which team serves first.
8. Hand a balloon to the team that wins the toss, and begin the game by tapping the balloon over the masking tape net.
9. Encourage the team opposite to tap the balloon back.
10. Take turns to serve the balloon to each other.
11. Try playing a game to fast music.

This page may be photocopied for instructional use only. *Themed Activities for People with Learning Difficulties* © M Hutchinson 2003

Speechmark

RECORDING SHEET 4

THEME: TAKE A BALLOON
Interactive Group Games – Table Balloon Tennis

Name: ______________________ Date: ______________

FOCUS OBJECTIVES	OBSERVATIONS AND COMMENTS
To encourage participation in group activities	
To develop spatial awareness	
To develop numeracy skills	
To develop hand-eye coordination	
To develop turn-taking skills	

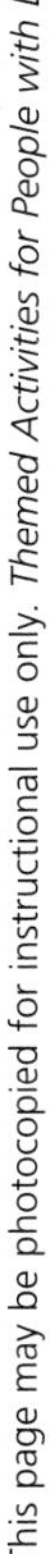
This page may be photocopied for instructional use only. *Themed Activities for People with Learning Difficulties* © M Hutchinson 2003

COMMUNICATION:
Basic Literacy

- Choose a short poem from a poetry book, or write your own poem
- Read through the poem several times
- Tap out the rhythm of the words in the poem
- Make a list of descriptive words
- Write out and illustrate poem

DRAMA:
Improvisation

- Take main elements from poem and make backdrops and props
- Create atmosphere – eg, darken room, use coloured lights
- Choose characters or roles
- Improvise movements
- Act out poem as it is read out and music is played

Theme

Take a poem

PHYSICAL EDUCATION:
Movement

- Wear comfortable clothes
- Sit in a semi-circle on chairs or on mats
- Work through sequence of warm-up exercises
- Tap out the rhythm of the poem
- Reflect rhythm of poem in body movements
- Use parachute/large piece of material to exaggerate movements

MUSIC:
Incidental Music

- Listen to rhythm of poem
- Experiment with musical instruments to create sound effects, atmosphere, mood, etc
- Use instruments to represent characters
- Explore tempo and volume
- Use voices as well
- Accompany the performance of the poem

WORKSHEET 1 | THEME: TAKE A POEM

Communication – Basic Literacy

FOCUS OBJECTIVES

- To encourage self-expression
- To develop listening skills
- To develop fine motor skills
- To practise literacy skills
- To have opportunities to make choices

EQUIPMENT

Selection of poetry books
Sheets of paper and pen
Flip-chart or large sheets of paper and thick felt pen
Small drum and beater/tambourine
Magazines
Scissors
Glue stick

METHOD

1. Look through a selection of poetry books – read out some poems.
2. Choose a short poem from one of the books, or write a poem – this could be on an individual basis or as a group.
3. Read the poem out loud several times.
4. Tap out the rhythm of the words in the poem using a drum, a tambourine, a foot, a knee or clapping hands.
5. Make a list of the descriptive words in the poem.
6. Draw or find pictures of the descriptive words on the list.
7. Write the poem on a large piece of paper.
8. Cut out the drawings and pictures.
9. Glue the pictures or drawings around the words to illustrate the poem.
10. Repeat the process if more than one poem is chosen or written.

Speechmark P This page may be photocopied for instructional use only. *Themed Activities for People with Learning Difficulties* © M Hutchinson 2003

RECORDING SHEET 1

THEME: TAKE A POEM
Communication – Basic Literacy

Name: Date:

FOCUS OBJECTIVES	OBSERVATIONS AND COMMENTS
To encourage self-expression	
To develop listening skills	
To develop fine motor skills	
To practise literacy skills	
To have opportunities to make choices	

This page may be photocopied for instructional use only. *Themed Activities for People with Learning Difficulties* © M Hutchinson 2003

WORKSHEET 2

THEME: TAKE A POEM
Drama – Improvisation

FOCUS OBJECTIVES

- To develop purposeful movement
- To encourage self-expression
- To develop listening skills
- To develop choice and decision-making skills
- To encourage participation in group activities

EQUIPMENT

Poetry books
Art materials – old sheets, paint, card, boxes
Scissors
PVA glue/glue sticks
Lamps with different coloured bulbs
Power-breakers
Recorded music and tape recorder
Selection of musical instruments
Flip-chart or large sheets of paper and thick felt pen

METHOD

1. Look through the poetry books and choose a short poem.
2. Read the poem.
3. Make a list of the main elements in the poem – eg, animals, underwater, cold, hot, people, in a forest, etc – on the flipchart or paper.
4. Decide what needs to be made – scenery, costumes, props.
5. Create an atmosphere – darken the room, use coloured lights, fans, sound effects, and material as backdrops, etc.
6. Choose characters or roles.
7. Work through some warm-up exercises – for example, lifting shoulders up and down, lifting arms up and down, shaking hands, tapping or stamping feet.
8. Read the poem out loud, and improvise actions and movements.
9. Play recorded or live music during the performance.
10. Encourage individuals to initiate movement and to direct the improvisation.

Speechmark This page may be photocopied for instructional use only. *Themed Activities for People with Learning Difficulties* © M Hutchinson 2003

RECORDING SHEET 2

THEME: TAKE A POEM
Drama – Improvisation

Name: ______________________ Date: ______________________

FOCUS OBJECTIVES	OBSERVATIONS AND COMMENTS
To develop purposeful movement	
To encourage self-expression	
To develop listening skills	
To develop choice and decision-making skills	
To encourage participation in group activities	

Speechmark  This page may be photocopied for instructional use only. *Themed Activities for People with Learning Difficulties* © M Hutchinson 2003

WORKSHEET 3 | THEME: TAKE A POEM
Physical Education – Movement

FOCUS OBJECTIVES

- To develop choice and decision-making skills
- To encourage turn-taking
- To encourage peer group interaction
- To develop purposeful movement
- To maintain and develop mobility

EQUIPMENT

Large pieces of paper and a thick felt pen
Mats or chairs
List of warm-up exercises
A short poem
A small parachute or large piece of material
Comfortable clothes

METHOD

1 Write the list of exercises and the poem on large sheets of paper.
2 Put them up on the wall.
3 Sit in a semi-circle – on mats or chairs.
4 Work through a sequence of warm-up exercises twice – for example, rolling head from side to side, shrugging shoulders up and down, shaking hands, lifting arms up and down, stamping feet.
5 Go round the group and tap out the syllables in each person's name.
6 Read through the poem twice.
7 Tap out the rhythm of the poem – on knees.
8 Repeat the poem – clap, stamp, sway to the rhythm.
9 Spread out a parachute or piece of material in a circle.
10 Encourage each person to hold the piece of parachute or material in front of them.
11 Lift the parachute/material up and down to exaggerate the rhythm of the poem.

 This page may be photocopied for instructional use only. *Themed Activities for People with Learning Difficulties* © M Hutchinson 2003

RECORDING SHEET 3

THEME: TAKE A POEM
Physical Education – Movement

Name: ____________________ Date: ____________________

FOCUS OBJECTIVES	OBSERVATIONS AND COMMENTS
To develop choice and decision-making skills	
To encourage turn-taking	
To encourage peer group interaction	
To develop purposeful movement	
To maintain and develop mobility	

Speechmark This page may be photocopied for instructional use only. *Themed Activities for People with Learning Difficulties* © M Hutchinson 2003

WORKSHEET 4

THEME: TAKE A POEM
Music – Incidental Music

FOCUS OBJECTIVES

- To encourage participation in group activities
- To develop hand-eye coordination
- To develop awareness of self and others
- To encourage self-expression
- To develop listening skills

EQUIPMENT

Poem – written on a large sheet of paper
Selection of percussion instruments – drum, tambourine, ocean drum, bells, shakers
Electric keyboard
Power-breaker
Tape recorder and blank tape

METHOD

1. Read out the poem.
2. Listen to the rhythm of the poem.
3. Clap and stamp out the rhythm.
4. Experiment with the musical instruments to see what sounds they make.
5. Use the instruments to represent characters, atmosphere, and mood in the poem.
6. Explore tempo – read out the poem at different speeds, and play instruments at the same rate.
7. Look to see if there are quieter or louder parts to the poem.
8. Use the instruments to represent the louder and quieter parts of the poem, by hitting or shaking them louder or more quietly as the poem is read out.
9. Accompany a performance of the poem with recorded and live music.

This page may be photocopied for instructional use only. *Themed Activities for People with Learning Difficulties* © M Hutchinson 2003
Speechmark

RECORDING SHEET 4

THEME: TAKE A POEM
Music – Incidental Music

Name:

Date:

FOCUS OBJECTIVES	OBSERVATIONS AND COMMENTS
To encourage participation in group activities	
To develop hand-eye coordination	
To develop awareness of self and others	
To encourage self-expression	
To develop listening skills	

This page may be photocopied for instructional use only. *Themed Activities for People with Learning Difficulties* © M Hutchinson 2003

THE ENVIRONMENT:
Sounds

- Make a list of different sounds – eg, voices, machines, water, animals, cars, etc
- Put tape into tape recorder
- Practise using the machine
- Choose 10 sounds from the list and record them
- Listen to recordings

MUSIC:
Looking at Instruments

- Choose 10 instruments
- Find pictures of each instrument
- Cut out and glue to large piece of card
- Number instruments on poster
- Record sound of each instrument
- Use tape and poster together as resource

Theme

Take a tape recorder

COMMUNICATION:
Interviews

- Choose a topic for the group to discuss – eg, favourite food, colour, football team
- Write down questions
- Choose who is to ask questions first
- Switch on tape recorder
- Record interviews
- Listen to recordings

INTERACTIVE GROUP GAMES:
Guess Who?

- Record each person vocalising/speaking
- Photograph each person
- Sit around a table
- Place photographs in the middle of the table
- Play one voice at a time
- Match the photograph to the voice

WORKSHEET 1

THEME: TAKE A TAPE RECORDER
The Environment – Sounds

FOCUS OBJECTIVES

- To develop an understanding of cause and effect
- To develop fine motor skills
- To develop recognition and matching skills
- To encourage turn-taking
- To develop listening skills

EQUIPMENT

Flip-chart or large pieces of paper
Thick felt pen
Tape recorder and blank cassette
Selection of environmental sounds – washing machine, telephone, car, kettle, radio, alarm clock, running tap, etc

METHOD

1. Spend time sitting and listening to sounds around you.
2. Write them down on a large piece of paper or flip-chart.
3. Add other sounds that you think of to the list.
4. Put a blank tape into the tape recorder.
5. Practise recording sounds on the tape recorder.
6. Switch the machine to record.
7. Clap hands, stamp feet, speak, shout, play a musical instrument.
8. Stop recording and rewind the tape.
9. Play back the recording.
10. Choose 10 sounds from your list.
11. Spend time recording each one.
12. Listen to the recordings.
13. Decide which ones are quiet, loud, fast, slow, etc.

Speechmark P This page may be photocopied for instructional use only. *Themed Activities for People with Learning Difficulties* © M Hutchinson 2003

RECORDING SHEET 1

THEME: TAKE A TAPE RECORDER
The Environment – Sounds

Name: ______________________ Date: ______________________

FOCUS OBJECTIVES	OBSERVATIONS AND COMMENTS
To develop an understanding of cause and effect	
To develop fine motor skills	
To develop recognition and matching skills	
To encourage turn-taking	
To develop listening skills	

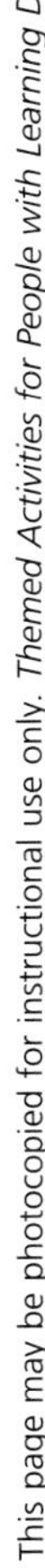
This page may be photocopied for instructional use only. *Themed Activities for People with Learning Difficulties* © M Hutchinson 2003

WORKSHEET 2

THEME: TAKE A TAPE RECORDER
Music – Looking at Instruments

FOCUS OBJECTIVES

- To encourage participation in group activities
- To develop hand-eye coordination
- To develop listening skills
- To have opportunities to make choices
- To develop turn-taking

EQUIPMENT

Books and magazines containing information about musical instruments
Large piece of card
Sheets of paper
Scissors
PVA glue/glue stick
Felt pens
Tape recorder and blank tape
Selection of instruments – voice, tambourine, piano, drum, shaker, castanets, cymbal, guitar, recorder, wood-block, etc

METHOD

1. Look through the books and magazines for information about instruments.
2. Choose 10 instruments.
3. Find or draw pictures of each one.
4. Cut out pictures and glue on to a large piece of card.
5. Write a label for each instrument.
6. Number and label each instrument on the poster.
7. Put the blank tape into the tape recorder.
8. Collect the instruments on the poster.
9. Take it in turns to play the instruments – record as you go.
10. Use the tape and poster together as a resource.

Speechmark  This page may be photocopied for instructional use only. *Themed Activities for People with Learning Difficulties* © M Hutchinson 2003

RECORDING SHEET 2

THEME: TAKE A TAPE RECORDER
Music – Looking at Instruments

Name: ______________________ Date: ______________________

FOCUS OBJECTIVES	OBSERVATIONS AND COMMENTS
To encourage participation in group activities	
To develop hand-eye coordination	
To develop listening skills	
To have opportunities to make choices	
To develop turn-taking	

This page may be photocopied for instructional use only. *Themed Activities for People with Learning Difficulties* © M Hutchinson 2003

WORKSHEET 3

THEME: TAKE A TAPE RECORDER
Communication – Interviews

FOCUS OBJECTIVES

- To develop choice and decision-making skills
- To develop listening skills
- To encourage peer group interaction
- To develop literacy and numeracy skills
- To develop turn-taking skills

EQUIPMENT

Sheets of plain paper
Flip-chart or large sheets of paper and thick felt pen
Pen
Magazines – ideas for topics
Tape recorder and blank tape

METHOD

1. Choose a topic for the group to discuss – favourite food, pop stars, sport, fashion, etc.
2. Encourage each person in the group to think of a question to ask and write it down on a sheet of paper.
3. Use pictures, symbols, or objects of reference to allow everyone to think of a question.
4. Write each question on the flip-chart/large piece of paper.
5. Put a blank tape into the tape recorder.
6. Practise recording individual voices on the tape.
7. Choose who is to make the first interview.
8. Press record on the tape recorder, and record the first interview. Ask one person in the group the list of questions, allowing time for their replies.
9. Rewind the tape after all the recordings have been completed.
10. Play back the interviews to the group.

This page may be photocopied for instructional use only. *Themed Activities for People with Learning Difficulties* © M Hutchinson 2003

RECORDING SHEET 3

THEME: TAKE A TAPE RECORDER
Communication – Interviews

Name: ______________________ Date: ______________________

FOCUS OBJECTIVES	OBSERVATIONS AND COMMENTS
To develop choice and decision-making skills	
To develop listening skills	
To encourage peer group interaction	
To develop literacy and numeracy skills	
To develop turn-taking skills	

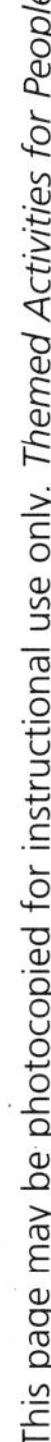
This page may be photocopied for instructional use only. *Themed Activities for People with Learning Difficulties* © M Hutchinson 2003

WORKSHEET 4

THEME: TAKE A TAPE RECORDER
Interactive Games – Guess Who?

FOCUS OBJECTIVES

- To develop awareness of self and others
- To develop listening skills
- To develop matching skills
- To develop turn-taking skills
- To encourage self-expression

EQUIPMENT

Camera and film
Large sheet of paper or plain material – background for photograph
Card
Scissors
Glue stick
Tape recorder and blank tape
Pen

METHOD

1. Secure the large sheet of paper or material to a wall or door.
2. Position a chair in front of the paper or material.
3. Take two portrait-style photographs of each person in the group.
4. Have the film developed and printed.
5. Encourage individuals to choose the photograph they like out of the two taken.
6. Glue the chosen photograph on to a piece of card.
7. Trim the card to leave a border around the photograph.
8. Put the tape into the tape recorder.
9. Record each person speaking, vocalising, laughing, etc.
10. Sit around a table.
11. Place the photographs in the middle of the table.
12. Play each voice on the tape one at a time.
13. See who can match the voice on the tape to the photograph on the table.

This page may be photocopied for instructional use only. *Themed Activities for People with Learning Difficulties* © M Hutchinson 2003

RECORDING SHEET 4

THEME: TAKE A TAPE RECORDER
Interactive Games – Guess Who?

Name: ______________________ Date: ______________________

FOCUS OBJECTIVES	OBSERVATIONS AND COMMENTS
To develop an awareness of self and others	
To develop listening skills	
To develop matching skills	
To develop turn-taking skills	
To encourage self-expression	

This page may be photocopied for instructional use only. *Themed Activities for People with Learning Difficulties* © M Hutchinson 2003

Appendices

Resources and Materials

Additional themes

Further themes are suggested in the list below. Photocopy the blank theme boxes on page 223 to develop chosen or original themes by thinking of four activities to explore.

- Colour
- Flowers
- Clothes
- Seaside
- Forest
- Buildings
- Transport
- Entertainment
- Fashion
- Food
- Animals
- Caves
- Plastic
- Wallpaper
- Box
- Windows
- Paper bag
- Newspaper
- Paper plate
- Farm

Finding materials

The list below will give you ideas about where to find materials. Individual groups will have additional sources to utilise.

- Charity shops
- Scrap projects
- Budget shops
- Large companies
- Wood yards
- Factories
- Magazines – specialist, general
- Libraries
- Bookshops
- Markets
- Recycle or adapt materials you already have

Further Reading

Allen C (ed), 2001, *A Framework for Learning – for adults with profound and complex learning difficulties*, David Fulton Publishers Ltd.

Aziz K, 1991, *The Encyclopaedia of Indian Cooking*, Bloomsbury Books.

Bennett J & Millar A, 1998, *Bright Ideas – Festivals*, Scholastic Publications Ltd.

Berriedale-Johnson M, 1995, *Sainsbury's Special Diets Cookbook*, HarperCollins.

Black P, 1993, *Cards and Collages*, Ebury Press.

Edden G (ed), 1992, *The Good Housekeeping Step-by-Step Cook Book*, Colour Library Books Ltd.

Fitzjohn S, Weston M & Large J, 1999, *Festivals Together – A Guide to Multi-Cultural Celebration*, Hawthorn Press.

Grau A, 1998, *Dance*, Dorling Kindersley Ltd.

Lambe L & Hogg J, 2000, *Creative Arts – and people with profound and multiple learning disabilities: education, therapy and leisure*, Pavilion Publishing (Brighton) Ltd.

Montgomery D, Rawlings A & Hadfield N, 1994, *Bright Ideas – Lifesavers*, Scholastic Publications Ltd.

Newton-Cox A & Beverley D, 1997, *Making Birdhouses*, Lorenz Books.

Otten L (ed), 1999, *A Curriculum for Personal and Social Education*, David Fulton Publishers Ltd.

Park L, 1987, *Art Attack – Programmed art for the frenzied teacher*, Ashton Scholastic.

Spurgeon T (ed), nd, *Getting on with Gardening – A book for people with sight loss*, Royal National Institute for the Blind.

Theme Boxes

Theme

This page may be photocopied for instructional use only. *Themed Activities for People with Learning Difficulties* © M Hutchinson 2003

CHECKLIST FOR ACTIVITIES

ACTIVITY:	Yes	No	Comments
1 · Who is the activity for? An individual A small group A large group			
2 · Are focus objectives being highlighted?			
3 · Is there adequate space for the activity?			
4 · Are all the relevant materials and equipment needed for the activities available?			
5 · Does the activity need to be broken down into smaller steps?			
6 · Is there enough time to complete the activity in one block of time?			
7 · Are there any adaptations that need to be made to materials and equipment?			
8 · Will individuals need to be positioned in a particular way during the activity?			
9 · Will individuals be involved in setting up, participating in and clearing away?			

Speechmark P This page may be photocopied for instructional use only. *Themed Activities for People with Learning Difficulties* © M Hutchinson 2003

ACTIVITY PLAN

Time	ACTIVITY:	Aims	Resources

This page may be photocopied for instructional use only. *Themed Activities for People with Learning Difficulties* © M Hutchinson 2003

INDIVIDUAL RECORDING SHEET

THEME: ____________________

Name: ______________________ Date: ______________________

FOCUS OBJECTIVES	OBSERVATIONS AND COMMENTS

This page may be photocopied for instructional use only. *Themed Activities for People with Learning Difficulties* © M Hutchinson 2003

GROUP RECORDING SHEET

THEME: ____________________

Group members: ____________________ Date: ____________________

FOCUS OBJECTIVES	OBSERVATIONS AND COMMENTS

This page may be photocopied for instructional use only. *Themed Activities for People with Learning Difficulties* © M Hutchinson 2003

Speechmark

EVALUATION SHEET FOR ACTIVITIES

ACTIVITY:	Yes	No	Comments
1 · Was the activity appropriate?			
2 · Were any highlighted focus objectives achieved?			
3 · Was the activity set up and presented appropriately?			
4 · Was there enough space for the activity?			
5 · Was the activity broken down into small enough stages?			
6 · Was there enough time for the activity?			
7 · Were any adaptations to materials or equipment successful?			
8 · Were students involved in all parts of the activity?			
9 · Are there any changes that need to be made for next time?			

This page may be photocopied for instructional use only. *Themed Activities for People with Learning Difficulties* © M Hutchinson 2003